Where's the Party?

Where's the Party?

In Relation to the Ten Commandments

By

Bill Hawkins

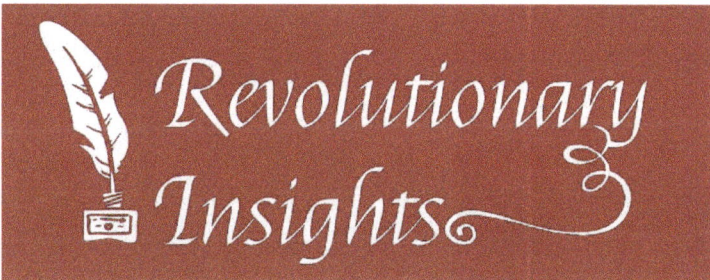

ISBN: Softcover   978-1-7357405-0-8
ISBN: E-Book   978-1-7357405-1-5

Printed in the United States of America

Edited by H.C. Bowen

Cover Design: D. J. Kuhns

Scripture Quotations of King James Version taken from
https://www.kingjamesbibleonline.org

Revolutionary Insights
Acknowledgements

Romans 8:28: *"And we know that all things work together for good to them that love God, to them who are the called according to [his] purpose."* As a result of the time God had granted me due to losing my job as a result of COVID-19, I was able to start "Revolutionary Insights," which included publishing two new books, starting a podcast, and becoming a speaker in churches. I would like to thank my wife Sherry for encouraging me to start the new venture because she thought I had something to say due to the insights she said God had given me.

D. J. Kuhns was also a big help as he had been after me for years to start a podcast. He had the equipment and the experience to convince me to move forward. He also designed the covers for my last two books.

Mark Holowchak, perhaps the world's leading authority on Thomas Jefferson, has also been invaluable by reading my manuscripts and offering suggestions which were greatly appreciated.

I would also like to thank members of my family for their help and encouragement during this process. My sister Kathy did a great job designing graphics. My daughter Heather helped with editing and my son Logan and daughter Anna listened to me for years, not always willingly, as I honed my knowledge and insights on the topics of history, politics and the Bible.

Other Books by Bill Hawkins

Prickett's Fort – A frontier novel set on the Appalachian frontier of 1778. Based on two true stories. A family friendly novel.

Inside the House of David – A commentary on II Samuel which covers the time in David's life when he was King of Israel.

Revolutionary Insights Podcast – Commentary on the three areas of Christianity, Politics and History.

www.revoltionaryinsights.com

Table of Contents

Preface

In 1976 my family moved from West Virginia to Florida when I was 14 years of age. It was time for the Presidential election where Jimmy Carter, the Democrat, was facing Gerald Ford, the Republican. I watched the Democrat National Convention because I was curious about the future of the nation that I was going to inherit.

I assumed I was a Democrat. I recall in fifth grade the teacher explaining the difference between the Democratic and Republican Parties. "Democrats are known for being liberal, or progressive. Republicans are known for being conservative, meaning they don't like change." A student asked what progressive meant and the teacher answered, "Progressive means you are for progress and conservative means you're against progress." Another student asked, "Isn't progress good?" She answered, "Yes, progress is good."

Therefore, using what she said and combining it with the fact that the word liberal sounded like the word liberty, I reasoned I must be a Democrat. Still, I wasn't sure, so I asked my mom when I got home what the difference was between Democrats and Republicans and she answered that Democrats were for the poor and Republicans were for the rich. I knew we more poor than rich, so I again concluded I was a Democrat.

As I sat watching the '76 Democrat National Convention, I was excited to see the Democratic champions who were fighting for the people of this nation. However, the more I watched the more concerned I became. I grew up believing in God, patriotism, and a sense of self-reliance. I began to worry for my country as the Democrats talked about their platform. The thought came to me, "If the Democrats are this bad, then how bad are the Republicans?!"

A week or so later the Republican Convention took place and I contemplated not watching because I feared the Republicans would be much worse than the Democrats. However, I've always been the type of person that wanted to hear both sides of the story in order to get as much information as possible before I decide. So, I swallowed hard and sat down to watch the Republican National Convention.

What I saw was hope. I saw respect for God and a desire to do right. I saw a love for country, a desire to preserve the good, and hope for a better future. I saw the value that was placed on individual liberty and the belief that people could be trusted to know what was best for them. That message resonated with me.

As I watched the Republicans adopt their platform, I remember being excited and jumping up from where I was sitting, walking into the kitchen and asking, "Mom, did you know that we're Republicans?"

She turned and looked at me with surprise and asked, "Is there a difference?"

"Oh my, yes," I replied, and then added, "The difference is huge!"

Ever since that evening, I have wondered how good Christians could support a party that fought against everything they believed. "Why?" I'd ask myself. To me and many other Christians, the difference was plain. I wanted to help people see the differences between the parties and what they envisioned for the future of this country. But how could I do that?

I recently prayed about it and this thought came to me, "Simply show where the parties stand in relation to the 10 commandments."

So, I did, and the results were surprising even to me.

When I sat down to write this book, I thought one party would probably support six or seven of the commandments and the other two or three. However, once I studied the party platforms, policies, and writings, I realized the differences were even greater than I imagined.

The first three chapters of this book, *Where's the Party?*, discuss the role of Christians in politics and whether we ought to participate, or to abstain from entangling ourselves with the world. Political philosophies are then addressed along with the political wheel to give the reader a clear understanding of the direction politicians are taking us. Within the church we have doctrines which frame our beliefs and the reader will see how political correctness has become the doctrine of the left as they attempt to force us to accept their idea of government.

The next 10 chapters each address one of the 10 Commandments through a study of party platforms, writings and actions. As a result, readers will see the position of the Democratic and Republican Parties in relation to the 10 Commandments making the differences between the two parties sufficiently clear so we can rightly choose the party Christians are to support if they put God's law above man's law.

The final chapter looks at the question of truth. How important is truth? Can we know truth and what do we do when confronted with it? Is the real answer to the state of our nation political, or will it be found elsewhere?

Once these questions are answered, it's then up to you, the reader, to help preserve the nation God gave us.

Chapter 1

In the Beginning

Would Jesus have been a Democrat or Republican? Should Christians be in politics? Does it matter where the two major political parties in America stand in relation to the Ten Commandments?

Let's answer those questions, which will help us to understand the importance of this book when it comes to seeing the truth of what is happening in America where the government and churches are concerned. Let's look at the first question: Would Jesus have been a Democrat or Republican? The answer is simple enough because he would not belong to either party. How do I know this? Because he did not belong to any party or faction when he walked the earth 2,000 years ago.

At one point in Luke 20:22, the Pharisees asked, *"Tell us therefore, What thinkest thou? Is it lawful to give tribute unto Caesar, or not?"* They were trying to put Jesus in a difficult position by asking if it was lawful for a Jew of Israel to bow to a man, Caesar, by giving him tribute. After all, weren't the Jewish people only to bow to God and not to be a respecter of persons as it says in Proverbs 28:21, which reads, *"To have respect of persons is not good: for for a piece of bread that man will transgress"?*

Jesus knew they were trying to trap him and called them hypocrites. He dumbfounded their scheme by replying in Luke 20:23-25, *"But he perceived their craftiness, and said unto them, Why tempt ye me?*
24 Shew me a penny. Whose image and superscription hath it? They answered and said, Caesar's.
25 And he said unto them, Render therefore unto Caesar the things which be Caesar's, and unto God the things which be God's."

This was the first time the concept of separation of church and state was uttered. Jesus was saying that the government has its place, which is to govern man. God also has his place, which is to oversee his creation. It all belongs to him. He just allows some to govern at his pleasure. Daniel 2:21 says, *"And he changeth the times and the seasons: he removeth kings, and setteth up kings: he giveth wisdom unto the wise, and knowledge to them that know understanding:"*

What does this tell us about the question that asks if Jesus would have been a Democrat or a Republican? It tells us that Jesus, the Son of God, came to earth not to be a King of Israel, but to be the King of Kings. As Jesus said in Luke 17:20-21, *"And when he was demanded of the Pharisees, when the kingdom of God should come, he answered them and said, The kingdom of God cometh not with observation:*
21 Neither shall they say, Lo here! or, lo there! for, behold, the kingdom of God is within you."

God's kingdom is spiritual and not physical. Government is man's attempt to control his environment, whereas, the Kingdom of God is not of our environment. Therefore, Jesus would not have entangled himself with the physical world since he was only concerned with the spiritual.

This brings us to the second question: Should Christians be in politics? Ideally, it would be great if Christians stayed out of politics and concentrated only on being a good Christian. Unfortunately, history tells us that the government, when operating outside of the principles of God, becomes an enemy of Christians, sometimes going so far as to kill them. Christians have the right of self-defense, and a Christian lawfully participating in government is akin to practicing self-defense.

In America we have a constitution, which begins in the preamble with three particularly important words . . . "We the people . . .."

"We the people" means that our government belongs to the people. The government derives its power from the people, and that means it's up to the people to participate and guide the government to protect us all from those that might try to change our government and take it in a direction that would enslave the people to the government. If Christians participate in our government, which is our right, then the interests of Christians can be protected from anyone who would use our government to persecute us for our beliefs.

Christians are to be motivated by love when dealing with our fellow man, whether Christian or not. If I love my family, my community, and my nation, I will want what is best for them. When Biblical principles are practiced in any of those three arenas, then good things happen. When those principles are abandoned, then we see bad things happen, such as an increase in crime, lawlessness, and corruption. Love for our fellow man means maintaining Biblical principles for the benefit of everyone.

A scoffer may ask, "But aren't Christians supposed to follow the example of Jesus and not become entangled with the world of politics?" To answer that question, we must look at the purpose of our being here in the first place. Jesus Christ came to earth for the purpose of redeeming mankind. He lived his life a perfect man without once sinning. He took our sins upon him when they nailed him to the cross, and he willingly gave his life for us so that those who acknowledge their sins and trust in his sacrifice can then be redeemed and be given a spiritual life, which allows us to enter heaven upon our death.

The purpose of Christians is different than the purpose of Jesus Christ. Our purpose is to point to the death, burial, and resurrection of Christ as the only way to heaven and a life more abundant while here on earth. We are to show that God's way is best for the individual, his family, his community, and his nation. That means we operate on Biblical principles for ourselves, our family, our community, and our nation. Therefore Christians are supposed to participate in politics, even if just by voting in a Godly manner. We do so to show that God's way is the best way and that he loves us and wants the best for us.

We are blessed to live in the United States of America, which gives each citizen the right to govern by voting for leaders and by participating as government leaders if called by God.

Does it matter where the two major political parties in America stand in relation to the Ten Commandments? Allow me to ask that question another way. Does it matter whether Christians support Godly or evil principles? Of course, it matters.

Does it matter to God? If you doubt whether good government matters to God, then read the book of Judges. There you will see that good government that follows Godly principles does indeed matter to God.

Judges 2:10-16 - *"And also all that generation were gathered unto their fathers: and there arose another generation after them, which knew not the LORD, nor yet the works which he had done for Israel.*

11 And the children of Israel did evil in the sight of the LORD, and served Baalim:

12 And they forsook the LORD God of their fathers, which brought them out of the land of Egypt, and followed other gods, of the gods of the people that were round about them, and bowed themselves unto them, and provoked the LORD to anger.

13 And they forsook the LORD, and served Baal and Ashtaroth.

14 And the anger of the LORD was hot against Israel, and he delivered them into the hands of spoilers that spoiled them, and he sold them into the hands of their enemies round about, so that they could not any longer stand before their enemies.

*15 Whithersoever they went out, the hand of the LORD was against them
for evil, as the LORD had said, and as the LORD had sworn unto them: and
they were greatly distressed.
16 Nevertheless the LORD raised up judges, which delivered them out of
the hand of those that spoiled them."*

When the government became corrupted because they had forgotten the
ways of God, turmoil began in their nation. God cared so much for his people that he sent a deliverer. Those deliverers, or judges, restored the government as a Godly one.

Whatever political party you belong to, keep in mind, I'm speaking of political parties and not its individual members. Not everyone believes right down
the line what their party believes and supports. As Christians, we are to be
sure that we are in line with the Word of God. Our party is to be in line with
the Word of God as well. If it's not, then we need to find one that is and
then support that party because it's more important to be in line with God's
Word than it is a party platform. If our opinion differs from God's, then it's
our opinion that needs to change.

If you are not a Christian, read this book with your eyes open and not as a
member of a political party or adversary. Find out what Christians believe
and not just what non-Christians teach you we believe.

We all have a choice as to what we believe - Christian and non-Christian. It
is important for us to keep in mind the consequences of our beliefs. Are we
making the world a better place for our family, communities, and nation, or
are we following an ideology that is trying to exploit our weaknesses so that
we can be ruled?

The choice is yours. Choose wisely.

Chapter 2

The Political Wheel

Before we go any further, it would be best to start this book by defining in as clear a way as possible the differences between liberalism, leftism, fascism, socialism, and communism. Each of these political philosophies are based on the belief that government is good and solves problems. They also, to some degree, reject the Judeo-Christian ethic, and they are also all forms of socialism to varying degrees. So, it behooves us to know what is behind these political philosophies.

The remaining political philosophy in America, not mentioned above, is conservatism. It is often misunderstood because the practitioners of socialism have mis defined it, yet because they control so much of our education system and media, people have been duped into believing it is something it is not.

Therefore, in order to make this book truly effective, we need to start at the foundation and build our way up so that by the time we get to the chapters on the Ten Commandments, you will understand not only the what, but more importantly, the why.

There are two basic philosophies in America upon which political parties stand. Those two philosophies are known as secular humanism and the Judeo-Christian ethic. secular humanism, hereafter simply called humanism, is as much of a faith as Christianity. The United States Supreme Court has identified humanism as a religion in Torcaso v. Watkins from 1961. https://caselaw.findlaw.com/us-supreme-court/367/488.html

Since then, they have dropped religious language from their writings so they can be the lone "religion" taught in our public schools.

To show you just how entrenched humanism has become in America and how it achieved such a stranglehold, let us look at John Dewey, who is known as the Father of Modern Education. http://www.onthew-ing.org/user/Edu_Dewey%20-%20Father%20of%20Modern%20Educa-tion.pdf He's also the chief designer of the 1933 edition of the *Humanist Manifesto*. The following are a few of the tenets of humanism. https://amer-icanhumanist.org/what-is-humanism/manifesto1/

- Humanists regard the universe as self-existing and not created, and mankind is evolving toward a higher plane of existence.
- Humanists do not believe in an afterlife and instead believe that ful-fillment is in the here and now.
- Humanists reject traditional religion and find their religious emotions expressed in a heightened sense of personal life and in a cooperative effort to promote social well-being.
- Humanists believe capitalism needs to be replaced through a radical change in methods, controls, and motives. A socialized and cooper-ative economic order must be established, and wealth redistribution established. The individual is deemphasized in favor of the govern-ment.

Since humanists reject the idea of God, then it follows they must reject the Bible, which is known as the Word of God. If the Word of God is to be rejected, then right and wrong need to be redefined because the Bible serves as the basis of law in Western Civilization. https://creation.com/the-christian-foundations-of-the-rule-of-law-in-the-west-a-legacy-of-liberty-and-resistance-against-tyranny

This is done through what is commonly called situational ethics, meaning right and wrong are determined by the individual based on the situation. Mo-rality is thus redefined, and because government becomes the highest power instead of God, right and wrong are then determined by the government and can be everchanging.

As a result, the biggest enemy of humanism is Biblical Christianity.

Biblical Christianity is known as the Judeo-Christian ethic. Judeo refers to the Old Testament and Christian to the New Testament. A person who believes in the Judeo-Christian ethic does not have to be a Christian. That person simply believes that history has proven Biblical principles to be the most effective way to govern.

The Judeo-Christian ethic says,

- God created the universe and mankind and rejects the theory of evolution.
- Heaven and Hell are real places and an afterlife exists.
- God is worthy to be worshipped and His Word followed. The Bible defines morality in the Ten Commandments and in other passages of His Word.
- Free enterprise and capitalism is the most effective and fair economic system because it values the individual and what he earns he is allowed to keep.

The best way to illustrate the differences in modern political systems is through the political wheel I have developed over years of study and observation. Instead of thinking of left and right on a linear spectrum, which is the usual way people attempt to determine political differences, I believe it is best to look at politics as a wheel.

The linear system presents problems when determining where some people or political systems would fall on the spectrum. For example, just before WWII people were surprised that Adolph Hitler and Joseph Stalin could sign a treaty since they were on opposite ends of the political spectrum. Stalin being Far Left and Hitler Far Right. However, when we look at their location on the political wheel, we will see that they weren't on opposite ends of anything because they were bosom buddies in the zone labeled Despots.

While Stalin's government resided in the communism zone and Hitler's in the fascist zone, they both shared socialist ideas. Their countries were rivals, but the leaders were ruthless despots that used their political philosophies to do what all despots do - rule as dictators.

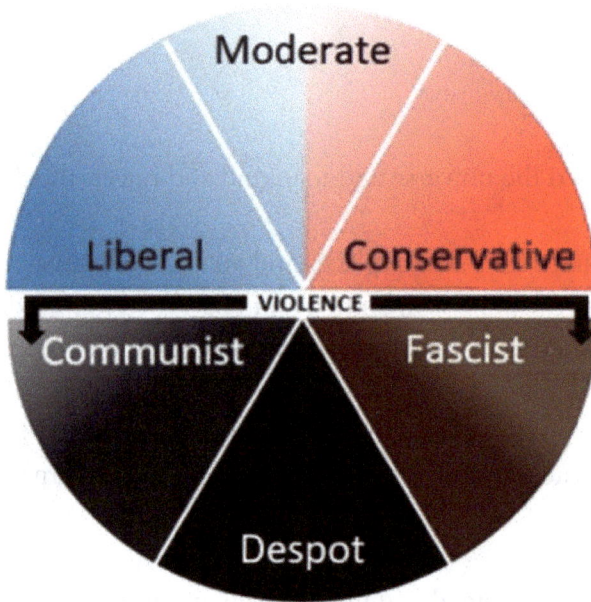

Fig. 1. The upper half of the Political Wheel is where the United States traditionally has operated in the 20th and 21st Centuries. Our two political parties are marked by blue for the Democrat Party and red for the Republican Party. Notice the gradient of color changes as it becomes more or less extreme. The lower half of the Political Wheel shows the dominant political philosophies of the last hundred plus years and gets darker as the violence needed to maintain power becomes more brutal. The gap separating the

political philosophies is labeled violence because the bottom half is where a population is controlled through threats or acts of violence.

The upper half of the wheel is where the United States Political System operates. This half does not use violence to rule over the people; instead, we contract together under our constitution to pursue the best for ourselves and our neighbors. The lower half is where violence and force is used to coerce people to obey their government or intimidate factions attempting to overtake the government. The dividing line between violence and non-violence is a big gap because to cross it takes a big step.

The location of an individual or nation on the wheel will give you a good idea of where that person or nation stands. For example, the Republican Party operates on the upper-right side of the political wheel in the conservative zone. The Democrat Party operates on the upper-left side of the political wheel in the liberal zone. In between reside those who are called moderates.

The libertarian, another political philosophy of America, concurrently resides in two zones, being both conservative and liberal. The libertarian's distrust of government is shared with the conservative's, whereas the libertarian's moral stance has more in common with the liberal's.

What is the difference between liberals and leftists? Most people would think there is no difference because the left has co-opted the name liberal. The truth is, the classic liberal used to run the Democratic Party, but recently, the left has taken over the Democrat Party from the classic liberals and continues to be swept left as if caught in a raging torrent. Truth be told, the classic liberal has much more in common with the right than they do the left.

The left in America is best explained as communist. On the political wheel, they fit into the communist zone better than they do the liberal zone. The reason they were hard to identify in the past was because they resided in the liberal zone since they did not practice violence. However, probably the greatest triumph of President Trump was angering the left (communists) so much that they had to come out in support of violence. The leadership of the Democrat Party has failed to seriously renounce violence out of either fear of the left or because the leaders themselves are leftists.

For example, take a look at these quotes:

"If you see anybody from [the Trump] Cabinet in a restaurant, in a department store, at a gasoline station — you get out and you create a crowd. And you push back on them. Tell them they're not welcome anymore, anywhere!" - Maxine Water (D) CA

"When they go low, we go high. No. When they go low, we kick them." - Eric Holder, former Democrat Attorney General under Obama

"You cannot be civil with a political party that wants to destroy what you stand for, what you care about. That's why I believe, if we are fortunate enough to win back the House and or the Senate, that's when civility can start again. But until then, the only thing that the Republicans seem to recognize, and respect is strength." - Hilary Clinton, former Democratic Presidential candidate.

The riots of May and June 2020, which the Democrats for the most part appear to support by not denouncing or attempting to stop, are another example of what the left might call "acceptable violence." Even the Democrat leaders who say they oppose the riots also say it's understandable and give them free reign to burn and loot.

On July 2, 2020 Sen. Mike Lee of Utah introduced a non-binding resolution that offered a statement of support for peaceful protesters and law enforcement who do their job well, while condemning violence and the desecration of monuments across the country.   Democrats blocked the resolution. https://thefederalist.com/2020/07/02/democrats-block-resolution-condemning-mob-violence/

The box below compares conservatives, classic liberals, and leftist so that we can more readily see the differences of each political philosophy. You will see that the classic liberal has much more in common with conservatives than leftist.

Issue	Conservative	Classic Liberal	Leftist
Race	Color is insignificant. Oppose forced segregation	Color is insignificant. Oppose forced segregation	Color is significant, and those that disagree are racist. Support segregation in some instances
Capitalism	Support; less government control	Support; more government control	Oppose; supports socialism
Nationalism	Supports nation-states; closed borders	Supports nation-states; closed borders	Oppose, preferring citizens of the world; open borders
America	Patriotic	Patriotic	Sees America as the problem and socialism as the answer
Free Speech	Supports	Supports	Opposes, identifying any speech they do not agree with as hate speech
Western Civilization	Supports	Supports	No better and a form of white supremacy

https://www.prageru.com/video/left-or-liberal/

13

The political philosophy some think has been quietly nipping at the heels of our nation for over a century is socialism. However, truth be told, socialism has not been nipping at our heels, it has taken a big chunk out of us to the point where our country is in mortal danger.

In 2016 Bernie Sanders ran openly as a socialist within the Democratic Party. If not for the Democrat Party rigging the election in Hilary Clinton's favor, it is possible that one of our two major political parties would have nominated an open socialist for the highest office in the land. https://www.independent.co.uk/news/world/americas/us-politics/donna-brazile-hillary-clinton-dnc-primary-rigged-bernie-sanders-a8034716.html

Socialism takes up half of the political wheel, with nearly the entire lower half being consumed by that philosophy. As you see in Fig. 2, the dividing line of socialism cuts midway through the Liberal and Fascist zones.

So let's talk briefly about the lower half of the political spectrum, which is dominated by socialism. The three zones on the lower half are Communism, Despot, and Fascism. Communism uses the government to attempt to control every aspect of society, including the people living under communist rule. There is one political party, and it holds all power over the country, economy, and people.

The Despot zone is inhabited by dictators who use the government to try to control their country and people. Monarchs of old could fall into this zone, pulling their country in after them even if the country's government isn't recognized as completely socialist.

Fascism seems harder to define, only because Hitler gave it such a bad name. Too many people don't want to be honest about what Fascism really is because of its socialist component. Fascism is a combination of nationalism and socialism, which is usually controlled by a strong leader, ending up in the Despot zone.

Fascism does allow heavily regulated capitalism as long as the private owners of those companies support the state. When ownership of property is conditional on obedience to the state, then in reality, private property does not exist.

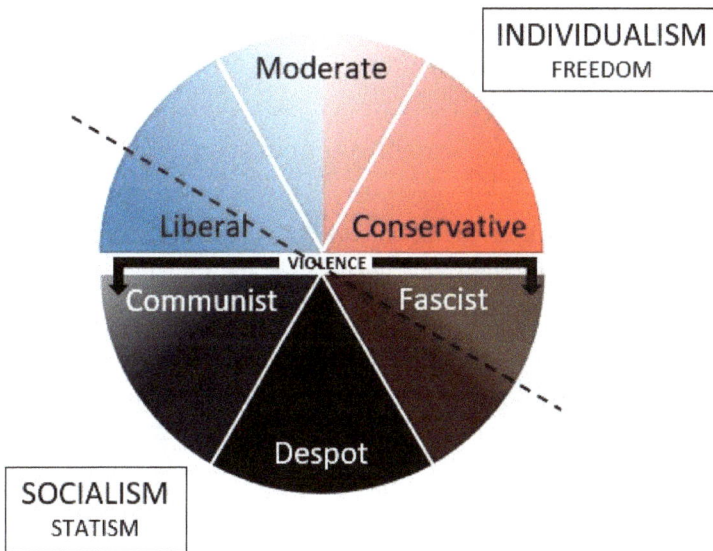

Fig. 2 - The dashed line that cuts through the Liberal and Fascist zones shows how socialism and statism lie below the dashed line, while individualism and freedom lie above the dashed line. As examples, NAZI Germany operated in the Fascist zone below the socialism line, and the USSR operated in the Communist zone well below the dashed line. Hitler and Stalin, however, both operated as individuals in the Despot zone. The modern Republican Party operates in the center of the Conservative zone and the Democrat Party operates in the Liberal zone and below the socialism line, dangerously close

to the violence gap as evidenced by the party's refusal to denounce the violence of leftist mobs.

Notice in fig. 2 that statism, power belonging to a highly centralized state, is below the violence gap because the only way the state can demand obedience is through the use of force. The opposite of statism is individualism, where in the tenth amendment, power is reserved to the states or to the people.

Leftists think fascism is like conservatism because of its nationalist component, and conservatives think fascism is like communism because of its socialist component. Truth is, fascism stands alone because the nationalism component is not like the nationalism of conservatism. The socialism component of fascism is not like the socialism of communism.

Let's take a closer look at nationalism so we can better understand why conservative nationalism is unlike fascist nationalism. I recently was talking to a man born and raised in Hong Kong who was asking me questions to clarify the differences between Democrats and Republicans. He seemed to have a mixture of the two and wasn't quite sure where he stood. During this conversation, he asked something that took me a minute to wrap my mind around because his way of thinking was so different. He thought nationalism and being a patriot was dangerous.

I identified the way he spoke as being a leftist thought, but I still didn't understand why the leftist thought love for country was dangerous. So I asked him to explain his thought process. He said it was because in Nazi Germany people who loved their country did horrible things to their enemies, both foreign and domestic. He went on to say that Kamikaze pilots in WWII dove their plans on suicide missions into American ships out of love for their country. So what is to stop an American who loves his country from also committing heinous acts of brutality against enemies both foreign and domestic?

That was a very good question, and a few years ago, I would have answered his question differently, but now, because of the violence coming from the left that is not being condemned by Democrats, I had to agree that it could happen in America too.

I asked him if he was a Christian, and he said he was. So I asked him which laws Christians are to obey first: God's laws or man's laws? He said Christians are to obey God's laws first. I then asked if God's laws would permit us as individuals to commit heinous acts against our enemies both foreign and domestic. He said no. To which I asked, "Which political party has as their basic core belief morality as defined in the Bible?" He answered, "The Republican Party."

I then asked which political party in American was currently carrying out acts of violence against those they disagree with. His reply was the Democratic Party. I asked him why that was, and he wasn't sure at first, then answered, "Because they don't base their morality on the Bible." I agreed; the morality of the Democratic Party is based on humanism, which says that morality is defined by the individual and society.

The reason leftist teach that nationalism and patriotism is bad is because they oppose the constitution of our country and they want to destroy it so that a socialist utopia can come to America. To a leftist, people who love America are the enemies, therefore, patriotism must be denounced.

America saved Europe and the Pacific region during WWII, and we have been a force of good in the world by fighting tyrants and those who would destroy their own people. We did so because we had as our core belief the Bible and its morality.

However, as the Democrat Party has abandoned those beliefs and turned wholeheartedly toward humanism and socialism, we do have reason to fear what could happen should they come to power again because they do not have a higher moral authority than that defined by society and thus the government, which they would control.

Americans used to wonder how Adolf Hitler and the Nazi's could come to power in Germany. The German Worker's Socialist Party (Nazi) came to power because they bullied and intimidated their enemies into silence. Does that sound familiar? It should because the same thing is beginning to happen in the United States of America!

What needs to be understood is that fascism exists below the violence gap of the political wheel, along with communism. Another way of saying this is that fascism controls with the fist and communism with the gun. A fascist will beat you up and shut down your business; whereas a communist will shoot you and take your business.

The end goal of socialism, whether in its communist or fascist form, is to create a utopia. A heaven on earth where we all get along peaceably, and all our problems are solved by the government.

The end goal of humanism is the belief mankind will continue to evolve until we reach perfection and become gods.

Of course, for either socialism or humanism to succeed, they must first destroy whatever is in the way of their end goal. That is why the left fights God, Christianity, and capitalism, which values the individual.

Chapter 3

Political Correctness

At what age does a person know the difference between right and wrong? In religious circles, this is known as the age of accountability. Legally, there is no standard definition, but one of the questions asked as to when people can be declared legally insane is "Do they know the difference between right and wrong?"

However, what is more important than knowing the difference between right and wrong is knowing who defines right and wrong.

Lawmakers should be the first people that come to mind when answering that question, but how do lawmakers choose what is right and wrong? Is it a mere matter of a majority vote? If the majority votes to legalize murder, does that mean murder is no longer morally wrong?

This brings us to the even more important questions: Who defines morality? Why is murder wrong? Why is stealing wrong? Is it a simple matter of anything that harms another is wrong? If so, then why is it wrong to commit suicide?

Traditionally in western cultures, right and wrong is based on the Judeo-Christian ethic - in other words, the Bible, both Old and New Testaments.

However, what happens when someone chooses not to believe the Bible? More importantly, what happens when millions of people choose not to believe the Bible? Are they then held to the standards of a book they don't believe has any authority?

As long as lawmakers make laws based on the moral authority of the Bible, then those people have to conform, or else they would be committing a crime. So then, how would these millions get themselves out from under a morality they don't believe in because they choose not to accept the authority of the book that morality is based upon?

The obvious answer is that they create their own standards of right and wrong based on what a few leaders convince the majority to believe. They do this through controlling education, the media, and popular culture so they can elect lawmakers who share their belief that morality is situational to be determined by society and not the Bible.

Which brings us to another question: How do they determine what society believes morally when it's not based on the historical tradition of the Judeo-Christian ethic?

In religion, the standards of belief are known as doctrine. Merriam-Webster defines doctrine as a principle, or position, or the body of principles in a branch of knowledge or system of belief. Conservatives hold to the historical tradition of the Judeo-Christian ethic. Leftists do not accept the authority of the Bible and are attempting to destroy that historical tradition through their own doctrine known as political correctness.

What then do the liberals, or socialists, hold to as doctrine? Some would say the *Communist Manifesto* since it is a form of socialism; however, it is an extreme form that perhaps most socialists would say went too far. Is there a book the liberals can turn to?

The answer is yes; it's called the *Humanist Manifesto*. This is the same book that John Dewey, that some call the Father of Modern Education, helped humanists to create as they laid out their vision for America.

That does not mean the *Humanist Manifesto* is a book of doctrine any more than the Bible is a book of doctrine. The doctrine of churches or their belief system is based on teachings within the Bible. The doctrine of leftism, or socialism, is based on the principles as defined in the *Humanist Manifesto*.

You may better understand the doctrine of the left as political correctness. Merriam-Webster defines political correctness as conforming to a belief that language and practices which could offend political sensibilities should be eliminated. Whose political sensibilities are being offended? The sensibility of the left is the answer to that question. They are offended by the Judeo-Christian ethic.

Political correctness is couched in the emotional issues of fairness and helping those who cannot help themselves because they are dominated by the majority. Of course, that's what the left uses to shame anyone who opposes their doctrine by calling them hate mongers and insensitive to the rights of others. However, is that what political correctness is all about? Making right past wrongs?

No, because to support political correctness is to be insensitive to the rights of those who hold to the Judeo-Christian ethic. It can even be said that the politically correct crowd hates the Judeo-Christian ethic because before it can be replaced, it must be destroyed in order to be replaced with the doctrine of political correctness and eventually socialism.

Therefore, the question of who defines our morality becomes even more important because there is a concerted effort to destroy our historical tradition based on the Bible. What does history tell us about attempts to destroy the Judeo-Christian ethic?

They tried it in France in 1789, and it became known in history as The Reign of Terror when 50,000 people were executed for opposing those who abolished Christianity and tried to destroy all aspects of it from public life.

They tried it in Russia in 1917 and imprisoned people deemed enemies of the state. It is estimated that 60 million Russians under communism died in the attempt to destroy the Judeo-Christian ethic.

They tried it in Nazi Germany where nine million people, of which six million were Jews, were executed in an attempt to advance the socialist state of the German Workers Socialist Party or Nazis.

They tried it in China, to destroy their own historical traditions, and are still trying it to the tune of killing an estimated 40 million citizens of China.

Not all socialist countries kill their enemies (citizens who disagree), but they do deny their rights, marginalize them, or imprison them and attempt to re-educate them.

In this book, I will compare the Ten Commandments of the Judeo-Christian ethic with the doctrine of political correctness so we can see just how much the left is opposed to traditional morality and why.

That way, in case you don't already know, you can determine where your political party is and then either support it or abandon it. Whichever choice you make, if you're a Christian, be sure the party reflects your Christian values as defined by the Word of God.

Chapter 4

First Commandment

The Constitution of the United States of America was ratified in 1789. It defined our government and the foundation on which it stands. Which begs the question, what role does the Ten Commandments play in that government given to us by our founding fathers? Are they really the basis of law in America? To answer that question, one need look no further than the Supreme Court of the United States.

The Supreme Court Building has at the center of the sculpture over the east portico an image of Moses holding the two tablets of the Ten Commandments; these are also engraved over the chair of the Chief Justice and on the bronze doors of the Supreme Court.

The left has been trying, through our courts, to have the Ten Commandments removed from public buildings, saying that it violates separation of church and state, which incidentally, the left has created as the basis of their assault on Christianity by implying it violates the Constitution, when separation of church and state isn't even in the Constitution!

If our country was not founded on the Ten Commandments and Judeo-Christian Ethic, then upon what other philosophy was it founded? Could our great nation have been founded on humanism, or the idea that God's laws did not pertain to man? How could that be when humanism and socialism didn't exist in 1789! Darwin hadn't yet written the *Origin of Species*, nor had Marx written *The Communist Manifesto*. The *Humanist Manifesto*, which derived out of those two books had not yet been written. Therefore, the laws of Western Civilization were based on the Ten Commandments, and the Constitution of the United States was no exception.

Let's look at why the Democratic Party, who hosts liberals, socialist, leftists and communists, opposes the Ten Commandments one commandment at a time, beginning with the first commandment.

The first commandment says, *"I am the Lord thy God, thou shalt have no other gods before me."* (Exodus 20:3)

The left rejects God and in his place has established government as the highest authority over mankind.

What about liberal Christians who regularly attend church? God addresses this in II Timothy 3:5 when he says, *"Having a form of godliness, but denying the power thereof: from such turn away."*

A person becomes a Christian when they ask for God's forgiveness and accept the Lord Jesus Christ as their Savior. That is how the Bible says a person must be saved and therefore become a Christian. *"That if thou shalt confess with thy mouth the Lord Jesus, and shalt believe in thine heart that God hath raised him from the dead, thou shalt be saved."* (Romans 10:9)

Liberal "Christians" often either deny the deity of Jesus Christ or deny the power of God. Either way, they are either not Christians or they have been led astray as it says in verse 6 of II Timothy chapter 3: *"For of this sort are they which creep into houses, and lead captive silly women laden with sins, led away with divers lusts,"*

The second part of the First Commandment says *"thou shalt have no other gods before me."* The left, however, has established the government as its god. Why? Because when a person denies God, the highest authority becomes man, meaning the institution that governs man becomes in essence, god.

The first two tenets of humanism as defined in the *Humanist Manifesto I* say, "Religious humanists regard the universe as self-existing and not created. Humanism believes that man is a part of nature and that he has emerged as the result of a continuous process." https://americanhumanist.org/what-is-humanism/manifesto1/

Since humanism is not based on truth as defined by God, then truth can be ever-changing to a liberal. To account for this, humanists recognizing that fact update their beliefs as they change. Still, in the *Humanist Manifesto III*, published in 2000, they continue to hold to an unguided process of change and deny the existence of God. https://secularhumanism.org/index.php/1169

One thing that hasn't changed and seems to be a core belief of the left is that there is no God or, at the least, they deny God's power in the governance of mankind.

You may know those first two tenets as evolution, which is the basic foundation of the left since it denies God and therefore establishes evolution to explain our origin. As a result, a political party's stance on evolution is a clear indicator on whether the party accepts or rejects the very first commandment of God.

Which political party in America supports evolution and fights to keep creation from being taught in our public schools? Yes, it's the Democratic Party. Making it clear that the Democrat Party rejects the first commandment of God.

Not all Republicans believe in creation, but what is sadder is that not all Christians believe in creation. We have been so indoctrinated by the left that they have convinced many people, who should know better, that the theory of evolution should be accepted, even though it's never been proven nor can be proven.

Where is the party?

The Republican Party has been the party that traditionally has fought to at least have creation taught in our government schools alongside evolution. Many members of the party, especially the religious right, believes in creation. Making it clear that the Republican Party accepts the first commandment of God.

The Democrat Party fights against creation being taught and insists that our children only be taught evolution in our public schools.

Keep in mind that evolution is a tenet of humanism, which has been declared a religion by the Supreme Court. Thus, for those who argue that creation should not be taught because it is a religious belief, so is evolution a religious belief of the humanist.

Now that you know where your party stands, where do you stand? Do you stand with or against God?

Chapter 5

Second Commandment

We are not to worship anything other than God. Whatever man puts his faith in and sets up as a supreme guide that influences his actions is what he worships. Therefore, the person who believes the highest authority we are answerable to is government, worships government. That includes the Christian that places the authority of government above the authority of God.

The Second Commandment simply states, *"Thou shalt not make unto thee any graven image, or any likeness of any thing that is in heaven above, or that is in the earth beneath, or that is in the water under the earth,"* meaning that we are not to have idols or anything else that we put before God. (Exodus 20:4)

It goes hand in hand with the first commandment with the difference being that the first commandment is speaking spiritually of God alone being worthy of worship; whereas, the second commandment is referring to the physical world and worshiping something man made or tangible, such as government.

Where do the two parties stand when it comes to God? On page ii of the 2016 Republican Party platform it states, "Every time we sing, 'God Bless America,' we are asking for help. We ask for divine help that our country can fulfill its promise. We earn that help by recommitting ourselves to the ideas and ideals that are the true greatness of America."

Conversely, the 2016 Democratic Party platform says on page 17, "Democrats know that our nation, our communities, and our lives are made vastly stronger and richer by faith in many forms and the countless acts of justice, mercy, and tolerance it inspires. We believe in lifting up and valuing the good work of people of faith and religious organizations and finding ways to support that work where possible."

The difference between the two platforms is the Republican Party turns to God for divine help for America and the Democrat platform says that faith comes in many forms and the government will help where possible. Where the Republicans seek God and his help, Democrats say there are many gods.

In the New Testament, Jesus had this to say about the second commandment. Matthew 22:37-39 says, *"Jesus said unto him, Thou shalt love the Lord thy God with all thy heart, and with all thy soul, and with all thy mind. This is the first and great commandment. And the second is like unto it, Thou shalt love thy neighbor as thyself."*

How do the two parties go about loving our neighbor? Notice that there is no financial litmus test on who we are to love. If we love our neighbor, it goes well beyond helping the poor. However, for the purpose of this chapter, let us limit our discussion to how the two parties help the poor.

First, let us realize there are two different definitions of poor we are dealing with here. The Bible defines a poor person as a person who cannot help themself. Specifically, the widow, fatherless, or physically handicapped. The Bible does not define the poor as someone who has less money or someone who lives under the government defined poverty line. The latter is how our government defines the poor. But since we are talking about the government, we will use the government's definition.

The question then becomes "Whose responsibility is it to help the poor?" Is it the individual's responsibility to help the poor, or is it the government's?

We can see how compassion is practiced by members of both parties by how they want to help the poor and less fortunate. Republicans tend to give of their own personal belongings to the needy without coercion and out of an inner motivation of compassion. Whereas, Democrats tend to believe the government needs to help the poor and needy, and to do so, they take, through taxation, what belongs to someone else and then redistribute it in an effort to help those below the poverty line or in need, as defined by the government.

In a nutshell, the conservative sees compassion as an individual choice. Whereas the liberal sees it as a collective and compulsory duty of our government.

Former President Barak Obama incorrectly used the Bible in an attempt to justify welfare programs to help those deemed poor by the government. He would say we are to be our brother's keeper, meaning, in a Democrat's way of thinking, that it is up to the government to provide for our needy brother.

The "brother's keeper" story is found in Genesis 4:9, and it is the story of Cain killing his brother Abel. When God inquired of Cain the whereabouts of Abel, Cain answered, *"I know not, am I my brother's keeper?"* Cain didn't ask God that question expecting the answer to be "yes." He knew the answer was "no" because he correctly knew that God never called us to be our brother's keeper. That phrase - "brother's keeper" - in today's parlance is akin to saying, "That's not my job." Cain was right; it wasn't his job. Biblically speaking, we are not our brother's keeper.

That doesn't mean we are cold and callous to those in need. Quite the contrary. It is part of our personal responsibility to help those in need. We are not to leave it up to the government.

When we believe it is the responsibility of the government to provide for the needy, we are transferring that responsibility from the individual to the government. That is a convenient way for the Democrat to say they care when, in reality, they don't care enough to do something themselves.

God says we are personally responsible to love our neighbor as ourselves. He doesn't say that the government is to love your neighbor. You are the one with that responsibility.

I am not my brother's keeper. I am my brother's helper in time of need.

The Democrat Party violates the second commandment because it denies God and places its faith in the government as demonstrated by their practice of using government welfare to fool people into thinking they are helping the poor. After all, which is more compassionate: the number of people a party can add to the welfare rolls or the number of people a party can free from the welfare rolls? Welfare keeps people where they are; it does not cause them to rise above their circumstances.

Keeping someone poor is not love.

Where is the party?

The Republican Party believes individuals are personally responsible to help those in need, but no one is coerced into doing so.

The Democrat Party believes it is the government's responsibility to help those in need and will take from others to do so.

Biblically, we as individuals are to help those in need. We can do so on our own or through the church. Nowhere does the Bible say it is the responsibility of the government to help those in need.

Now that you know where your party stands, where do you stand? Do you stand with or against God?

Chapter 6

Third Commandment

What does it mean to take the name of God in vain? It seems by most church standards all that means is we are not to say "G__ d___." At one time in this country, that was a rare combination of words to hear, but presently it has become a common form of speech. However, is that all it means in Exodus 20:7 when it says, *"Thou shalt not take the name of the LORD thy God in vain; for the LORD will not hold him guiltless that taketh his name in vain"*?

Taking the name of the Lord in vain is much more than using profanity. When you take something in vain, you are saying it has no power, that it means nothing, that it is useless. The name of God is invoked, but since the person invoking it doesn't believe in God's power, that person is giving lip service to God. Giving lip service to God is breaking the Third Commandment.

In chapter 5, I compared the 2016 platforms of the Republican and Democratic Parties and discovered that the latter referred to many gods in their platform. In that same chapter, I also mentioned how the Democrats believe the highest authority in our lives is government. Titus 1:16 states, *"They profess that they know God; but in works they deny him, being abominable, and disobedient, and unto every good work reprobate."*

Let's use former Vice-President Joe Biden as an example of using the name of God in vain when he was asked for his stand on abortion and faith during the 2012 Vice-Presidential debates. His response was, "My religion defines who I am." He then went on to talk about how he has been a practicing Catholic his whole life and that he accepts his church's doctrine that life begins at conception, then added, "... I refuse to impose that on others."

How is it logical that our public and private beliefs on such a life and death issue can differ? If Joe Biden really believed his church's doctrine as he said, then he would support his church over his party. However, he stated he believed it was wrong to impose the will of God on people who don't believe like him. Since when is God's will an imposition that can be ignored?

He began his statement on abortion by saying, "It has particularly informed my social doctrine. Catholic social doctrine talks about those who, uh, who uh, can't take care of themselves."

I ask you, who is less able to take care of themselves than a baby in the womb?

The reason Joe Biden and other Democrats claim to be religious yet oppose the will of God is because they really do not believe in the power of God. They simply give God lip service, as Joe Biden did during the debates.

Isaiah 29:13 says, *"Wherefore the Lord said, Forasmuch as this people draw near me with their mouth, and with their lips do honour me, but have removed their heart far from me, and their fear toward me is taught by the precept of men:"*

In the Democratic Party, the precept of men says that the most defenseless human on this earth can be legally murdered. If they truly feared God, they surely would not support taking the life of a baby.

Let's go back to the 2012 Democratic National Convention and revisit the time half the delegates booed God. Did the 2012 Democratic Convention really boo God? The truthful answer is at least half, if not more, of the delegates did boo the failure of the chair to remove the mention of God from the platform. The voice vote was too close to call, but the chair called it anyway so that God was reinserted back into the platform after Democrat leaders had removed all mention of God previously.

Why would a political party not want to mention God in their platform? Not even a token mention of God . . .if a token mention of God by people who don't believe in the power of God could be seen as a classic example of taking the name of God in vain. And how much worse is leaving God out of the entire platform? That would have gone from giving God lip service to open hostility.

The Democratic Party platform of 2016 did manage to mention God three times, while the 2020 platform has reduced that number to one, but since the party has rejected God's Commandments, it's safe to say the Democrat Party has shattered the third commandment of God because they have moved from lip service to contempt. Any argument otherwise is merely an effort to deny the obvious in an effort to escape the truth.

Where is the Party?

The Republican Party honors God and asks for His help in the party platform.

The Democrat Party not only ignores God but shows open contempt for God and the Bible.

Now that you know where your party stands, where do you stand? Do you stand with or against God?

Chapter 7

Fourth Commandment

The fourth commandment simply says, *"Remember the sabbath day, to keep it holy."* (Exodus 20:5)

The sabbath is actually on Saturday, not Sunday. The reason Christians worship and attend church on Sunday is because Jesus rose from the grave on the first day of the week (Mark 16:9) and Paul preached to the disciples on the first day of the week (Acts 20:7)..

Of the Ten Commandments, only nine of them remained in effect by being reconfirmed in the New Testament. Those nine instances can be found in Matt. 19:18 and Romans 13:9. The one missing is the sabbath, but let's not forget that in Matt. 12:8 Jesus said he is Lord of the Sabbath.

If you would like to read more about the sabbath, I encourage you to read the article by Matt Slick, which can be found at this address: https://carm.org/why-do-we-worship-sunday-instead-saturday

The principle of the sabbath, a day of rest, is something that many Christians still practice and something we used to practice in the history of our country. This principle means that, even though keeping the sabbath is not required of Christians, the idea of a day of rest is a sound principle for the health of the body, both mentally and physically. Therefore, this country had what was known as Blue Laws that reflected a belief in a day of rest. If you're unfamiliar with Blue Laws and if you're under 50 you just may be, then I suggest you read more about them at this address: https://en.wikipedia.org/wiki/Blue_laws_in_the_United_States.

Blue Laws were a nod of respect to Christianity and those who practiced it. At one time, the social norms frowned on doing business on a day that was seen as the day we were supposed to be in church. Even those who didn't go

35

to church had a respect for tradition and maintained the principle of the sabbath, even if they weren't Christians.

However, there have always been those who fought against Christianity and the people who practiced it; therefore, Blue Laws became a target. So who was it that worked to rid Blue Laws and the sabbath principle? An obvious culprit would be leftists who deny God and have no respect for anything that smacks of religion. However, all the blame cannot be placed solely on them. Blue Laws were repealed because society changed. It has been acknowledged by nearly everyone that liberalism has already won the cultural war. As churches sought to fit into this new world, instead of holding fast to Biblical principles, they compromised those principles in order to be accepted by those who already rejected them.

Where is the party?

As our culture changed nearly all the Blue Laws in America have been repealed. Republicans used to oppose their repeal, but even today, most Republicans do not see why we should keep them in place since this particular commandment was not reaffirmed in the New Testament.

The Democrat Party led efforts to repeal Blue Laws since they were seen to impose religion on those who did not believe, or practice religion and they wanted an extra day to shop if they wished.

Now that you know where your party stands, where do you stand? Do you agree with the principle of the sabbath that we need a day of rest, or are you offended by the connection to religion?

Chapter 8

Fifth Commandment

"Honour thy father and thy mother: that thy days may be long upon the land which the LORD thy God giveth thee." (Exodus 20:12)

The family unit is the most important organization known to mankind. Destroy the family, destroy the nation. Once the nation is destroyed, then it can be rebuilt in the image of those who govern after the fall. When communism took over China, there was a massive redistribution of, not just wealth, but families as well. They were split apart in order to achieve a political goal - the subjugation of the people to the will of the government.

Read what Karl Marx and Fredrick Engles had to say about the family in their *Manifesto of the Communist Party* from 1848.

> Abolition of the family! [...] On what foundation is the present family, the bourgeois family, based? On capital, on private gain. In its completely developed form, this family exists only among the bourgeoisie. But this state of things finds its complement in the practical absence of the family among the proletarians, and in public prostitution.

> The bourgeois family will vanish as a matter of course when its complement vanishes, and both will vanish with the vanishing of capital.

> Do you charge us with wanting to stop the exploitation of children by their parents? To this crime we plead guilty.

Frederick Engles goes on to write in his work *The Principles of Communism* the following about the family:

> What will be the influence of communist society on the family?

It will transform the relations between the sexes into a purely private matter which concerns only the persons involved and into which society has no occasion to intervene. It can do this since it does away with private property and educates children on a communal basis, and in this way removes the two bases of traditional marriage – the dependence rooted in private property, of the women on the man, and of the children on the parents.

Is there an attack on the family in America? Good people assume it must be absurd to think that an American political party would want to destroy the family. However, if that party wanted to create a socialist state where the government would in essence become our nanny, then it's not so absurd.

Recall that the two parties are built on the foundations of the Judeo-Christian Ethic (Republican) and humanism (Democrat). The Republican Party defines family the same way the Bible and tradition from throughout the history of the world has defined family. Namely, father, mother, children. Man, woman, child.

The Republican Party believes that parents have rights to their children and that they are responsible for their upbringing. The state is not to interfere in the family with the exception of making sure they are protected from threats within and without. Therefore, the policies of the Republican Party are to support the family and strengthen it wherever possible. Strong families make a strong community, which makes a strong nation.

In the words of the 2016 Republican Party platform,

> "Traditional marriage and family, based on marriage between one man and one woman, is the foundation for a free society and has for millennia been entrusted with rearing children and instilling cultural values."

The Democrat Party, as it has moved ever further left, has redefined the family as stated in their 2016 Democratic Party platform.

> "Democrats applaud last year's decision by the Supreme Court that recognized that LGBT people—like other Americans—have the right to marry the person they love."

Do you realize that we now have, for the first time in the history of the United States of America, two opposing rights? Freedom of Religion gives us the right to practice our religion without government interference, but if you go down just a few paragraphs in the Democrat platform, you will read the following:

> "We support a progressive vision of religious freedom that respects pluralism and rejects the misuse of religion to discriminate."

The Democrat Party REJECTS the "misuse" of religion to discriminate.

Read that again.

THE DEMOCRAT PARTY REJECTS THE MISUSE OF RELIGION TO DISCRIMINATE!

Our freedom of religion is now in direct conflict with LGBT laws, and if it were up to the Democrat Party, our religious beliefs will either have to change or we will be corrected however they wish until we conform and renounce what God's Word says about LGBT.

Before we get to that, let me remind you that it's imperative you understand what the Bible says about LGBT and how Christians are to respond to those who defend that lifestyle. Make sure you have an understanding of what Christians really believe and do not base your opinion of Christians based solely on what the left says Christians believe. You can download a very good free booklet from Focus on the Family by following this link. https://media.focusonthefamily.com/fotf/pdf/channels/social-issues/what-does-the-bible-say_final3.pdf?refcd=209501.

What does God say about the LGBT issue?

He says this in Genesis 19:4-9

4 But before they lay down, the men of the city, even the men of Sodom, compassed the house round, both old and young, all the people from every quarter:
5 And they called unto Lot, and said unto him, Where are the men which came in to thee this night? bring them out unto us, that we may know them.
6 And Lot went out at the door unto them, and shut the door after him,
7 And said, I pray you, brethren, do not so wickedly.
8 Behold now, I have two daughters which have not known man; let me, I pray you, bring them out unto you, and do ye to them as is good in your eyes: only unto these men do nothing; for therefore came they under the shadow of my roof.
9 And they said, Stand back. And they said again, This one fellow came in to sojourn, and he will needs be a judge: now will we deal worse with thee, than with them. And they pressed sore upon the man, even Lot, and came near to break the door.

Just as we have revisionists who try to change history, we also have revisionists who try to change the Word of God. To see revisionist arguments and the responses, follow the link above and look on pages 11 and 12.

Leviticus 19:20 states very clearly - "Thou shalt not lie with mankind, as with womankind: it *is* abomination."

Leviticus 20:13 - *"If a man also lie with mankind, as he lieth with a woman, both of them have committed an abomination: they shall surely be put to death; their blood shall be upon them."*

Does that mean that Republicans believe homosexuals should be executed? Certainly not! When Christ came, he fulfilled the law and completed the task of paying for the sins of breaking God's law. Homosexuality is still condemened in the New Testament as it says in Romans 1:26-32, *"For this cause God gave them up unto vile affections: for even their women did change the natural use into that which is against nature:*

27 And likewise also the men, leaving the natural use of the woman, burned in their lust one toward another; men with men working that which is unseemly, and receiving in themselves that recompence of their error which was meet.

28 And even as they did not like to retain God in their knowledge, God gave them over to a reprobate mind, to do those things which are not convenient;

29 Being filled with all unrighteousness, fornication, wickedness, covetousness, maliciousness; full of envy, murder, debate, deceit, malignity; whisperers,

30 Backbiters, haters of God, despiteful, proud, boasters, inventors of evil things, disobedient to parents,

31 Without understanding, covenantbreakers, without natural affection, implacable, unmerciful:

32 Who knowing the judgment of God, that they which commit such things are worthy of death, not only do the same, but have pleasure in them that do them."

The difference between the penalty for homosexuality in the Old Testament and the New Testament is in the New Testament the death sentence is carried out in eternal damnation and exclusion from heaven.

I Corinthians 6:9-10 - *Know ye not that the unrighteous shall not inherit the kingdom of God? Be not deceived: neither fornicators, nor idolaters, nor adulterers, nor effeminate, nor abusers of themselves with mankind,*
10 Nor thieves, nor covetous, nor drunkards, nor revilers, nor extortioners, shall inherit the kingdom of God.

I Timothy 1:9-10 - *Knowing this, that the law is not made for a righteous man, but for the lawless and disobedient, for the ungodly and for sinners, for unholy and profane, for murderers of fathers and murderers of mothers, for manslayers,*
10 For whoremongers, for them that defile themselves with mankind, for menstealers, for liars, for perjured persons, and if there be any other thing that is contrary to sound doctrine;
https://digitalcommons.liberty.edu/cgi/viewcontent.cgi?article=1180&context=sor_fac_pubs

We are to love sinners, and that includes the homosexual sinner. However, we are not to excuse their sin anymore than we are to excuse our own. Why do we love sinners? Because, *"For God so loved the world, that he gave his only begotten Son, that whosoever believeth in him should not perish, but have everlasting life."* (John 3:16)

Even though we deserve eternal damnation for our sins, God sent his son to pay for our sins and give us eternal life if we confess our sins and trust in Jesus Christ for our salvation. Because of that love, homosexuals are no longer under the death sentence since Jesus fulfilled the law and took the punishment for homosexuality when he died on the cross. God is giving those who commit sins that do not cause the death of an innocent person more time to accept his gift of eternal life.

LGBT rights, which conflict with the 1st Amendment right to freedom of religion, are only one way the left is tearing down the family. Below is a brief list of other ways the Democrat Party is breaking down the family.

- The Welfare system pays extra for women to have babies without a father in the home.
- Women's Rights groups say women don't need men and generalize that all men will use and mistreat the woman.
- Education has silently shifted from being answerable to parents until now they are only answerable to the state.
- Entertainment shows weak fathers and makes them out to be buffoons.
- Pop Culture says we should challenge authority, including parental authority.
- Men continue to be emasculated by some women's rights groups in a misguided attempt at equality.
- The left has removed corporal punishment from the homes and schools and labeled it abuse.
- The left has removed the father's rights when it comes to the issue of abortion.

The riots of 2020 highlighted the problem of the breakdown of the family in America, especially in the black community where 75% of children have no father in the home. The organization which received the most headlines and support from leftist institutions such as the media and the Democrat Party was Black Lives Matter. However, if you look on the Black Lives Matter website to find out what they believe, you will find the following statement, "We disrupt the Western-prescribed nuclear family structure requirement by supporting each other as extended families and 'villages' that collectively care for one another, especially our children, to the degree that mothers, parents, and children are comfortable." https://blacklivesmatter.com/what-we-believe/

Yes, Black Lives Matter calls for the destruction of the black family and the institution of communism, yet the Democrat leaders bowed their knees in support. https://shorefrontnews.com/2020/06/10/nadler-the-only-congressman-who-refused-to-get-on-his-knee-at-pelosis-blm-ceremony/

Where is the party?

The Republican Party 2016 platform says, "Strong families, depending upon God and one another, advance the cause of liberty by lessening the need for government in their daily lives. Conversely, as we have learned over the last five decades, the loss of faith and family life leads to greater dependence upon government. That is why Republicans formulate public policy, from taxation to education, from healthcare to welfare, with attention to the needs and strengths of the family." p. 31

The Democrat Party, on the other hand, says this in their 2016 platform. "We will fight to secure equal pay for women, which will benefit all women and their families, particularly women of color who are disproportionately impacted by discriminatory pay practices, and against other factors that contribute to the wage gap. And we will combat the discrimination they face on and off the job." p. 4

Nowhere does the Democratic Party platform address the family as a whole. Instead, it focuses on what the party will give by forcing businesses and taxpayers to give until it hurts. Therefore, the Republican Party stands in support of the 5th Commandment of God, while the Democrat Platform stands in opposition to God's Word and the 5th Commandment.

Where do you stand? With or against God?

Chapter 9

Sixth Commandment

Thou shalt not kill. (Exodus 20:13)

You would think that neither political party would violate this commandment. Sadly, that is not the case.

There are two controversial instances where the government has authorized the killing of a fellow human being - capital punishment and abortion. Interestingly, the parties stand on opposite sides for both issues.

Let's look at capital punishment first.

The first mandate of the government is to protect the people. Capital Punishment has been a tool used in America from its founding. The purpose of capital punishment is to protect the people, which again, is the first mandate of government. It is the government taking a life to protect a life. That sounds like a contradiction, but it clearly is not.

When a person commits such a heinous crime as to earn the death sentence, then the only way to ensure that person never kills again is to take that person's life before he or she has a chance to take another innocent life.

The Republican Party platform says the following on page 40:

> "The constitutionality of the death penalty is firmly settled by its explicit mention in the Fifth Amendment. With the murder rate soaring in our great cities, we condemn the Supreme Court's erosion of the right of the people to enact capital punishment in their states."

Some people who oppose capital punishment think this is a contradiction to Christianity. Does the Bible call for capital punishment?

"Whoso sheddeth man's blood, by man shall his blood be shed: for in the image of God made he man." (Genesis 9:6)

"And he that killeth any man shall surely be put to death." (Leviticus 24:17)

How are these Bible verses not a contradiction with Exodus 20:13?

In the first instance, God granted the government the power to take a life when an individual took an innocent life. After all, the purpose of government is to protect the people for the same reason a soldier who kills another person during war is also acting under the authority of the government and not as an individual. The soldier, or government agent, is not committing murder unless his actions are done outside of the authority of government.

Page 15 of the Democrat Party platform says, "We will abolish the death penalty, which has proven to be a cruel and unusual form of punishment."

What God has instituted for the protection of the innocent; the Democrats want to abolish for the protection of the guilty.

The other issue where government has granted the right to take a life is the issue of abortion. There is a constant running argument between those who support taking the life of an innocent child and those that want to protect that life. Therefore, there's no reason to repeat all those arguments one way or the other here, so I will try to keep this brief.

The Bible has this to say about children, born and unborn.
https://www.focusonthefamily.com/pro-life/what-the-bible-says-about-the-beginning-of-life/

46

"Thus saith the LORD, thy redeemer, and he that formed thee from the womb, I am the LORD that maketh all things; that stretcheth forth the heavens alone; that spreadeth abroad the earth by myself;" (Isaiah 44:24)

God formed us from the womb. Our physical life began inside the womb, not when we were physically born. We all have been alive from our day of conception, not our day of birth. Each time a baby is conceived, the creation process starts for that child until the process is complete and they are delivered into the world as a new creation.

"Before I formed thee in the belly I knew thee; and before thou camest forth out of the womb I sanctified thee, and I ordained thee a prophet unto the nations." (Jeremiah 1:5)

Some people believe that we are not viable human beings until after a certain period of development in the womb. However, God says here that BEFORE we were formed that God already knew us. God has known you from before you were even conceived! Think on that for a moment to get an idea of the immensity of God. He had set Jeremiah apart for His service while Jeremiah was yet growing inside his mother's womb.

"But when it pleased God, who separated me from my mother's womb, and called me by his grace," (Galatians 1:15)

We are a seperate life within our mother's womb. We are not part of our mother, or the woman's body because God separated us from our mother while yet in the womb. We weren't separated from our mother when the umbilical cord was cut, but while yet in our mother's womb, God separated us. A life taken before birth is a separate human life.

"And it came to pass, that, when Elisabeth heard the salutation of Mary, the babe leaped in her womb; and Elisabeth was filled with the Holy Ghost:" (Luke 1:41)

Elisabeth was six months pregnant when she heard Mary's greeting. Elisabeth heard the greeting, but John, while still in the womb, responded. John already had an innate knowledge of who he was going to be while yet in the womb.

"For, lo, as soon as the voice of thy salutation sounded in mine ears, the babe leaped in my womb for joy." (Luke 1:44)

The baby responded emotionally while yet in his mother's womb. He was not a collection of cells without value; he was a human being with emotions and a sense of his surroundings.

"If men strive, and hurt a woman with child, so that her fruit depart from her, and yet no mischief follow: he shall be surely punished, according as the woman's husband will lay upon him; and he shall pay as the judges determine." (Exodus 21:22)

If a baby in the womb is accidentally killed by someone, then that person is responsible and can be taken to court and punished. God values an unborn child.

"The fathers shall not be put to death for the children, neither shall the children be put to death for the fathers: every man shall be put to death for his own sin." Deuteronomy (24:16)

What about rape or incest? This is one of the emotional arguments for those who try to justify killing a baby in the womb. God addresses this emotional issue right here in Deuteronomy 24:16. A child is not to be put to death for the sin of the father. Rape is a heinous sin and deserves severe punishment, but that punishment is for the father, not the innocent child.

"And the LORD said unto him, Who hath made man's mouth? or who maketh the dumb, or deaf, or the seeing, or the blind? have not I the LORD?" (Exodus 4:11)

Today it's common practice to test to see if the baby in the womb might have any deformities or deficiencies so the parent can be informed and decide whether to kill their child to escape having a baby that might not be able to lead what is termed a "fulfilling life." God says he has made that baby in the womb, including those who have a deformity or deficiency. God did not make a mistake, and we are not to kill the baby.

"Woe unto him that striveth with his Maker! Let the potsherd strive with the potsherds of the earth. Shall the clay say to him that fashioneth it, What makest thou? or thy work, He hath no hands?
10 Woe unto him that saith unto his father, What begettest thou? or to the woman, What hast thou brought forth?
11 Thus saith the LORD, the Holy One of Israel, and his Maker, Ask me of things to come concerning my sons, and concerning the work of my hands command ye me." (Isaiah 45:9-11)

Even though God may have given us a handicapped child, we are not to question him and argue with God about what he did. Remember, every life is a gift, and we are not to question the creator of the gift.

"Lo, children are an heritage of the LORD: and the fruit of the womb is his reward." (Psalm 127:3)

Our reward is our children. A handicapped child is not a punishment, but rather, a blessing of God.

What about the person who has already committed this sin? Just like the rest of us, God has provided a way out for the sinner.

49

"In whom we have redemption through his blood, the forgiveness of sins, according to the riches of his grace;" (Ephesians 1:7)

"I, even I, am he that blotteth out thy transgressions for mine own sake, and will not remember thy sins." (Isaiah 43:25)

I have a very close friend that I learned had an abortion when she was younger. She was afraid to tell me because of how badly "Christians" treated her when she went to the abortion clinic. Remember, Christians, it is our job to show women seeking an abortion the love of Christ by giving that woman options, including help after the baby is born. This woman is now a Christian herself but was unsure where she should stand on the issue of abortion since she was guilty of that very same sin.

I told her I was not angry with her because we all sin and come short of the glory of God. Abortion is not the unpardonable sin; rejecting Christ as the Son of God is the unpardonable sin.

I asked her if she had asked God to forgive her of her sins? She said yes. So I told her that God had forgiven her sin and it was not being held against her. I asked if she had forgiven herself, and she said she had tried. So, I told her God had forgiven her, and as far as God was concerned, it's settled. I added, "I'm not mad at you. We all sin and you now know it was wrong, so forgive yourself because no one else is holding it against you."
Instead of trying to justify our sin or excuse them, why not simply ask God to erase your sins? After all, he's the judge, and he will erase it and forget all about it if we will simply confess and ask him to forgive us.

Where is the party?

The 2016 Republican Party platform has this to say: "The Constitution's guarantee that no one can 'be deprived of life, liberty or property' deliberately echoes the Declaration of Independence proclamation that 'all' are 'endowed by their Creator' with the inalienable right to life. Accordingly, we assert the sanctity of human life and affirm that the unborn child has a fundamental right to life which cannot be infringed. We support a human life amendment to the Constitution and legislation to make clear that the Fourteenth Amendment's protections apply to children before birth." p. 13

Conversely, the 2016 Democrat Party platform says, "We will support sexual and reproductive health and rights around the globe. In addition to expanding the availability of affordable family planning information and contraceptive supplies, we believe that safe abortion must be part of comprehensive maternal and women's health care and included as part of America's global health programming." p. 41

God instituted capital punishment, which the Republican Party supports, and he opposes killing unborn babies, which the Republican Party also opposses.

The Democrat Party has the opposite stance of the Bible on both issues. So, while the Republican Party supports the 6th Commandment, the Democrat Party stands in opposition to God and the 6th Commandment.

Where do you stand now that you know where your party stands? As a friend of God or an enemy?

Chapter 10

7th Commandment

"Thou shalt not commit adultery." (Exodus 20:14)

Neither platform addresses the issue of adultery. However, I believe we can discern the parties' stances using other means.

Adultery is a sexual sin that occurs when a married person engages in a sexual relationship with a person to whom he or she is not married. I believe it is safe to say that it is a prevalent sin of which the best of us could find ourselves guilty. After all, one of the greatest heroes of the Bible, King David, was guilty of adultery.

Scandals in the political world where a politician is caught having relations with someone other than their spouse are not uncommon. Those types of scandals happen on both sides of the aisle. The fact that they are scandals at all speaks to the fact that even those who reject the Ten Commandments still hang on to the truth of the seventh commandment, for the most part.

Yet, what was once a death sentence to a political career has now been normalized to the point that an adulterous relationship does not carry the stigma it once did in this country. That is evidenced by the Bill Clinton scandal with an intern during his Presidency. At the time, the Democrat Party defended the actions of their leader by saying, "Everyone does it" and "It's his private life, and we should stay out of it."

Adultery has been accepted to the point that it's not seen as such an egregious act as it once was. Now, it's only a scandal if the sexual sin was not consensual or if the guilty party can be labeled a hypocrite.

So let's take a look at what the philosophies behind the political parties tell us about where they might stand.

Humanism, the philosophy behind the Democratic Party, rejects the Ten Commandments, which means that their moral barometer must be based on something other than the Bible. As it says in the *Humanist Manifesto II* in the Third Tenet, "We affirm that moral values derive their source from human experience. Ethics is autonomous and situational needing no theological or ideological sanction. Ethics stems from human need and interest."

Since the left's moral barometer is based on the human experience, it simply means that if it can be justified, then it is permissible. Right and wrong is to be determined by the individual. Ironically, this is the only time that the left gives any power to the individual. However, keep in mind that the government ends up defining morality, so the idea of the individual defining their own morality is simply an illusion. For example, a person might justify killing someone else, but if convicted by a court, that person is still going to go to prison.

Speaking of conviction, is it against the law to commit adultery? That depends on what state you call home. As society has changed, so have the laws. As it says in a "Salon" article from May 6, 2019, "..., prosecutions for adultery and sodomy laws were basically unheard of since the 1960s." In the late 60's we had what is called in this country "The Sexual Revolution," brought to us by the left.

In that same article it goes on to say, "With the appointment of Brett Kavanaugh (and Neil Gorsuch before him), the balance between liberal and conservative justices has swung decidedly to the right. While this is great news for pro-lifers, it could be bad news for anyone who might want to have extramarital sex."

Reading that in reverse, as if Hillary Clinton had won the Presidency and then appointed liberal justices to the Supreme Court, that quote could have read, "While this is great news for anyone who might want to have extramarital sex, it could be bad news for anyone who might want to save a baby's life."

The Infidelity Recovery Institute says in an online article, "Up until the mid-20th century most US states (especially Southern and Northeastern states) had laws against fornication, adultery or cohabitation. These laws have gradually been abolished or struck down by courts as unconstitutional." https://infidelityrecoveryinstitute.com/u-s-a-laws-on-infidelity-and-adultery/

Liberal courts (Democrat) struck down adultery as unconstitutional, and as a result liberals are now afraid that a conservative court (Republican) might reverse those rulings and once again outlaw adultery as a defense of marriage and the Ten Commandments.

Where is the party?

We have already seen that the Republican Party holds firm to the Ten Commandments and honors God's Word as a party. Even though society has changed, and sadly that change too often includes churches, you can see above that there is still a remnant who honor the 7th Commandment, and that remnant is the Republican Party.

Conversely, we have also seen that the Democrat Party has shunned the Ten Commandments and rejects God's Word. We also see that through the courts they have undermined the Ten Commandments.

Now that you know where your party stands, where do you stand? Do you stand in support of God's laws or against God's laws?

Chapter 11

8th Commandment

"Thou shalt not steal." (Exodus 20:15)

Have you noticed a pattern yet? Do you think you have an idea of where your party stands?

Since I think you have a good idea of where the parties stand on the 8th commandment, I'm going to tell you a story so you can see how subtle the Democrats are at attacking the Ten Commandments.

While pursuing my degree in teaching at a public college, my parents' pastor gave me a book during my sophomore year, which I failed to read until after I had graduated. The title of the book was *The Religion of Secular Humanism and the Public Schools* by Homer Duncan.

I thought I knew about humanism and that I would recognize it when I saw it, so it was my pride that kept me from reading the book. Once I did read it, however, I was shocked to discover that not only was I taught humanism, but that I would have taught it myself unawares.

Let me give you an example of what I was taught to teach that would have broken down the 8th commandment and taught my students it was okay to steal.

As I started class, I would ask my students by a show of hands if it was okay to steal. About 70% of my students said it was wrong to steal, but most conceded it depended on the circumstances. I would then reply it was wrong to steal no matter the circumstances. That would provoke a discussion, and I would tell this story I was taught to teach in college.

Imagine you're the father of a family of three kids and a wife, but you're unemployed and homeless. You're living in a shack out in the woods a few miles out of town. All your food is gone and you're desperate, but you believe it is wrong to steal. So, you go to town looking for a job. Each place you go to says they don't need anyone, and by late afternoon, you're getting desperate because your kids don't have any food. As you're on your way back to your shack, empty handed and hungry, you pass one of the businesses you had approached earlier about a job. The owner had told you he was sorry, but he wasn't hiring. You see he still has his fruit stand in front of the store, and you spy some delicious looking apples sparkling in the sun.

You know it's wrong to steal, but your family is hungry, and you don't have anything to give them. You already asked the man for a job and he said no, but you notice no one is watching. So now you must make a decision. Is it okay to steal some apples to take back to your starving children, or should you pass them by and let your kids starve?

At this point, nearly all the students with the exception of usually one holdout would say they would steal the apples. The other ones who said it was wrong before, still thought it was wrong, but they would do it anyway to feed their kids. The one student who said he wouldn't steal was vilified by the others as uncaring.

That was the point that my college training taught me to stop because the students would have learned their lesson that right and wrong depended on the situation. However, that was the humanist, liberal, Democrat response, and I was none of the above. Therefore, I didn't end the story there as I was taught to by my humanist, liberal, Democrat professor.

I announced to the class that I would not steal the apples, and I actually did have children, so I knew very well the responsibility of a parent. The class would then get angry with me, thinking I was some uncaring fiend who refused to feed his children because of some antiquated "law" written thousands of years ago.

I would then explain to them that I had been taught to teach them that story because the people who came up with it were trying to break down their morals. I'd then say, "It seemed to work, didn't it?" That's when I would tell them I'm going to continue with the story so they could see what the proper response should be.

However, before I continued, I wanted to ask them some questions about the possible consequences of their justification of stealing the apples.

"When you get back to the shack and walk in, your kids will come running up to you and ask excitedly, 'Daddy, Daddy, did you get a job?'"
How do you answer? The class answered, "No."

Your kids would be disappointed and start complaining about being hungry, so then you would say, "Don't worry, I have five apples that I found." You'd then take them out of your pocket and put them on the table while you turned to help your wife pour glasses of water for the kids.

I'd then ask, "Do you think your kids bought your lie, or did they see through it?"

The class would respond, "They probably saw through it since kids often see through their parents when they're being lied to."

I'd then say, "While you were turned around helping your wife, one of the kids takes an extra apple, and when you turn back around, you notice only four apples on the table. What do you do?"

At this point the class would squirm and become silent. So, I'd continue, "It's going to be hard to punish your kid for stealing when they know you stole the apples yourself, isn't it?"

The class would shake their heads in the affirmative. I'd continue by asking, "When you stole those apples and brought them home to your family, what did you teach your children?"

The class would usually remain silent, so I'd answer the question for them. I'd say, "You taught your kids to steal, and then you lied to them. Now when your kids lie or steal, do you have the moral authority to correct them, or will they have contempt for any correction you may want to give them?"

The class would answer, "They're going to be mad at you if you try to correct them, and they're probably not going to really listen."

I would then say that it took a starving family to get you to steal, but what if one of your kids could justify stealing under less serious circumstances? I'd ask, "Did you just teach your kids to steal if they can justify it?"

The class would answer, "Yes," but then they'd say, "What else could they have done? After all, the family was starving."

I'd ask, "Would you like to hear what a person who truly believes it's wrong to steal would have done?"

They'd say, "yes," so I would continue the story from where I was taught to stop.

"I'm standing there in front of the apples, tempted to steal them and take them back to my starving family. However, I know it's wrong to steal. What do I do?"

Some in the class respond that I go back inside and ask for a job again, to which some in the class would scoff at that idea. I'd remind the class that the owner already told me he didn't have a job available. So now what? The class would be silent, so I'd continue.

"You'd go back inside the store to talk to the owner."

At this point some in the class would remind me the owner is not hiring, so talking to him would be a waste of time. They also didn't think he would just give me food because he was in business to make money. I'd agree with them and go on with the story.

You'd go up to the owner and say, "I know you don't have a job, but I'm not asking for one. I'm homeless, and I have a family living in a shack in the woods who is very hungry. I know you can't give me a job, but if I sweep your entire store out, could I have five apples to take back to them?"

I'd then ask the class, "What do you think he will say?"

They answered, "He'll hand me a broom?"

"Yes," I'd answer. Then I'd ask, "Will he watch you like a hawk?"

They'd laugh and agree he would. I'd say, "He'd better watch you like a hawk. Remember, just a few minutes ago, most of you were willing to steal from him."

An awkward smile of embarrassment would come across their faces, and I'd continue. "So you sweep the store, and you do a very good job for him. You'd then hand him back the broom, and he'd tell you wait for a minute while he got your food."

I'd ask, "Will he give you the apples?"

The class would answer he would, and some would say, "He'll probably give even more!"

I'd agree and continue my story. "The man gives you two bags of groceries along with milk, and then he asks about your kids. You tell them how old they are, and he includes some candy in the bags. You thank him profusely and go back to the shack. This time when you walk in, the same thing happens. The kids run up to you and ask, 'Daddy! Daddy! Did you get a job?'"

I'd answer, "No."

Then they'd ask, "Where did you get the groceries?"

"You'd then explain to the kids where you got the groceries while you turned to help your wife get the glasses for the milk I had earned. While you had your back turned, one of the kids steals a piece of candy." I'd pause and ask the class, "Did you teach your kid to steal?"

They'd respond, "No."

I'd say, "Since you hadn't taught them to steal, it probably wouldn't have happened, but let's say one of the kids stole some of the candy. Do you have the moral authority to correct whichever one stole the candy?"

The class would answer, "Yes!"

"And that, students, is why you don't steal."

Where is the party?

The Democrat Party espouses a philosophy that teaches that situation and circumstances determine right and wrong.

The Republican Party espouses the philosophy that "Thou shalt not steal."

Which scenario would you vote for? Stealing the apples or working for them? Do you stand with God or against God?

Chapter 12

Ninth Commandment

"*Thou shalt not bear false witness against thy neighbor.*" (Exodus 20:16)

Don't lie to further your cause. That sounds simple enough; however, to define a lie, you must first define truth. If truth is up to the individual, then we all have our own truth. If we all have our own truth, then if your neighbor can justify making an accusation or testifying falsely about something of which you have been accused, your neighbor can lie and feel he is doing nothing wrong.

Since we are speaking of political parties, let us look at how important truth is to Democrats when testifying under oath.

Bill Clinton was impeached for lying when under oath to a Federal Grand Jury and in a Federal Civil Rights Case. He gave false testimony concerning accusations made against him by women seeking justice for sexual assault. He was impeached by the Republican controlled House of Representatives but acquitted by the Democrat controlled Senate.
https://www.congress.gov/congressional-report/105th-congress/house-report/830/

The accusations made during these cases were substantiated, and it is true that Bill Clinton lied under oath. However, the Democrats failed to remove him from office because they reasoned that lying under oath in a case of a sexual assault nature was not an impeachable offense.

In 2019 the Democrat controlled House of Representatives impeached President Donald Trump, but he was acquitted by the Republican controlled Senate.

In this case, the only people caught lying were the Democrat representatives that impeached President Trump! The following article by Kayla Gowdy will show the instances of bearing false witness by the Democrats during the impeachment process.

https://www.foxnews.com/opinion/dems-10-biggest-lies-in-trumps-senate-impeachment-trialkayla-gowdy

> Lie: This impeachment process began after an anonymous whistle-blower filed a complaint through the proper channels within the Office of the Inspector General.

> Fact: An article published on Oct 2, 2019 by the New York Times proved Schiff received an early account of the whistleblower's complaint despite his persistent denial. This gave Democrats time to come up with an impeachment plan before any information was released to the public.

> Lie: Democrats began the impeachment hearings out of concern for the country and the Constitution.

> Fact: Time and time again Democrats have gone on the record proving their motivations for impeachment to be political.

> Rep. Al Green, D-Texas: "I'm concerned if we don't impeach this President, he will get reelected."

Rep. Alexandria Ocasio-Cortes, D-N.Y.: "[Impeaching Trump] is about preventing a potentially disastrous outcome [in 2020]."

Rep. Adam Schiff, D-Calif.: "The president's misconduct cannot be decided at the ballot box."

Lie: President Trump, during a phone call with Ukranian President Zelensky, asked for a personal favor.

Fact: Despite consistent false statements from Democratic Congressmen and members of the media, the released transcript of the call proved President Trump said, "I want you to do us a favor." The "us" refers to America, not his political campaign.

Lie: President Trump's unprecedented withholding of aid endangered the United States and Ukraine.

Fact: Not only did Ukraine receive its aid on time and in its entirety, but President Trump actually resumed granting foreign aid after President Obama ended the practice.

Lie: President Zelensky felt pressure from President Trump to investigate the Bidens.

Fact: President Zelensky addressed the issue with the American press, stating the call was "normal" and "nobody pushed" him to do anything for the aid.

Lie: House impeachment witnesses are first-hand evidence of a quid pro quo.

Fact: Of the impeachment witnesses brought by House Democrats, Gordon Sondland was the only one who spoke directly with President Trump regarding aid to Ukraine. He was clear the president told him, "I want nothing. I want no quid pro quo."

Lie: The whistleblower is non-partisan and can be completely trusted.

Fact: The Intelligence Inspector General found the whistleblower has "arguable political bias" against Trump and was not a primary source to the conversation, giving him no credible knowledge of the situation.

Lie: Hunter Biden and his work at Burisma are not relevant to the impeachment proceedings as he and former Vice President Biden did nothing wrong.

Fact: Back in 2014, multiple mainstream media outlets, including Time and CNN, reported on Hunter Biden joining the board of

Burisma, saying it gave off the appearance of corruption. Every witness House Democrats brought to testify in the open hearings echoed the same sentiment.

Lie: The House of Representatives approved a strong enough impeachment case for the Senate to vote to remove President Trump from office.

Fact: Immediately after the articles of impeachment were handed over to the Senate, Democrats began demanding new evidence and for more witnesses to be brought forward since their case was weak and without evidence.

Lie: There was an urgent need for impeachment.

Fact: After saying for months that impeaching President Trump was an urgent matter, Pelosi refused to send the articles to the Senate, unnecessarily delaying the trial.

Another near casualty of the Democrat's willful shattering of the 9th Commandment was the confirmation hearings of Supreme Court Justice Brett Kavenaugh in 2019. The Democrats were very fearful of this appointment because Kavenaugh is a Catholic who supports the Judeo-Christian ethic. To Democrats, that made him unfit for the Supreme Court because of their opposition to the Ten Commandments. As a result, the Democrats and their media allies (CBS, NBC, ABC, CNN, MSNBC, *The Washington Post*, *The New York Times*, etc.) launched an all-out assault on the nomination. They went so far as to bear false witness against him through women making false accusations.

Justice Kavenaugh was investigated seven times, including investigations into the accusations made by Democrats as a last-ditch effort to keep a Christian off the Supreme Court. After all was said and done, not only was no evidence found to back up the claims of any of the accusers, but four of the accusers were referred for criminal charges for making false allegations. Some of those referred have confessed to bearing false witness. https://www.washington-times.com/news/2019/oct/20/editorial-lies-and-the-kavanaugh-hearing/

There are many more examples of Democrats that violate the 9th commandment. For that matter, I'm sure a person can find examples of Republicans who have borne false witness. The difference is that the Democrat Party does it as a matter of furthering their leftist agenda.

The media, as mentioned above, is made up of leftists and has the same leftist agenda that pushes their ideology on America. Sadly, too many people still think they are as honorable as they used to be when their mission was to report the news. Their recent labeling as fake news has been well earned.

Former CBS News president Van Gordon Sauter had this to say concerning the state of journalism as it currently exists: "To many journalists, objectivity,

balance and fairness—once the gold standard of reporting—are not mandatory in a divided political era and in a country they believe to be severely flawed."
https://www.aim.org/don-irvine-blog/former-cbs-news-boss-journalism-has-become-the-clarion-voice-of-the-resistance/

If journalists spoke the truth, objectivity, balance, and fairness would not be an issue because truth is objective, balanced, and fair. However, because leftists and liberals believe truth is relative, we end up with a media that is flawed and severely slants their news coverage to the left - so much so that it has ceased to be news and has now become nothing more than propaganda.

Where is the party?

The Democrat Party rejects the 9th commandment and wholly embraces the situational ethics of Humanism.

The Republican Party rejects situational ethics and stands firm with the 9th commandment.

Which party do you support? Do you support the one who defends the 9th commandment, or the one who habitually breaks it because, to them, truth is relative?

Chapter 13

Tenth Commandment

"Thou shalt not covet thy neighbour's house, thou shalt not covet thy neighbour's wife, nor his manservant, nor his maidservant, nor his ox, nor his ass, nor any thing that is thy neighbour's." (Exodus 20:17)

To covet means to yearn to possess something that does not belong to you. It also means that we should not begrudge someone else's good fortune. When we think happiness is to be found in what someone else has that we want, we are setting ourselves up for major disappointment and the feeling that life is unfair and has to somehow be rectified. We become victims of our own device.

Capitalism tells us that we keep what we earn, and property is to be protected. Therefore, if we work hard to achieve our goals, we are allowed to keep the fruit of our labor and others are not allowed to take it from us just because they covet what we have due to jealousy.

Socialism says that those who earned what they have really didn't earn it and they are making a victim of you by taking advantage of your abilities. Therefore, it's up to the government to make things fair by taking what achievers have and giving it to you. After all, as they say, the achievers had unfair advantages, and they're no better than you.

The day before I was to teach socialism to my class, I would give them a quiz and go over it the next day. Students love to get a teacher on a rabbit trail, so they don't have to actually do the lesson planned for the day. So, I would let the students think I was on a rabbit trail as I went over the quiz so they would listen more intently - thinking they were fooling me into not teaching them a lesson.

I would start the class by writing all the quiz scores on the board from highest to lowest. Of course, I'd leave the names off so no one would be embarrassed, even though the students had a pretty good idea who got what score.

I'd then tell the students that the quiz scores were too low, so we had to do something about them. After all, too many students were not scoring high enough and a few had even failed. I'd tell them, "We have to get those failing scores up so no one fails."

I'd then act like I was in deep thought on how to solve the problem. Then, as if I had a eureka moment, I'd exclaim, "I have it! We'll take some points from the overachievers and give them to the ones who really need the points."

I'd then ask the classes permission to do so, paying particular attention to the achiever's body language. I could tell they didn't like the idea, but they went along with it because they didn't want to seem like they were greedy. Those that had failing grades thought it was a terrific idea and got a lot of enjoyment out of it.

So I'd start taking points from those who scored over 90 to give to those who scored in the 30's. The problem was, there were never enough points to take from the achievers to give to those who slacked. At this point, I'd ask if I could identify who got what score so I could negotiate directly with those from whom I needed to take points. The class would always agree, so I'd write down the name of the person beside their quiz score.

The original scores would look like this.
    97 - Sherry
    94 - Bobby
    92 - James

72

88 - Chanell
85 - Tanika
85 - Corey
81 - Brenda
77 - Missy
74 - Brenton
71 - Monique
70 - Sharon
62 - Maurice
54 - Jeff
50 - Carl
32 - Danny

I'd tell the class we needed to get Danny's score to at least a 70 so that he passed. I'd ask Danny if he minded if I took points from someone else to help get his score to a passing grade. He'd smile and say, "That's fine with me." He'd then laugh as he was enjoying the idea of not having to worry about passing or failing.

I'd then turn to Sherry and say, "Sherry, I know I already took 4 points from you so that you now have a 93 instead of a 97, but I'm going to need more points. I'm sure you won't mind because you'll still have an 'A.'"

Sherry's expression would be one of barely concealed anger, but she'd reluctantly agree. So, I'd say, "I'm going to need to take 3 more points from you to give to Danny. That will leave you with 90, which is still an "A."

Then I'd tell Bobby, "I need to take more points from you too. You're down to 92, so I've only taken 2 from you. I'm going to need to take 3 more from you which will leave you with an 89."

Bobby would then say, "But that will make me get a "B" instead of an "A."

"Yeah, well, it can't be helped. I've only been able to get Danny 16 extra points so far and that means he only has 48. We still have a way to go to get him to a passing grade, so I don't have much choice. Would you mind if I only take 3 points?"

Very reluctantly, Bobby would give me permission. Then I'd go down the list of scores, taking more points from those who had passing scores until I had to go back to Sherry at the top.

"Sherry, you still have more points than anyone, and I still need 9 more points to get Danny a passing grade. I'm afraid I'm going to have to take more points from you."

Sherry would be mad now and say, "That's not fair! I earned those points."

I'd reply, "Sherry, don't be greedy. You don't need all those points. Besides, you were born with a silver spoon in your mouth, and you have had unfair advantages. Why don't you like Danny, anyway? Is there something wrong with you?"

Of course, I was being sharp with her because I was showing the class the power of peer pressure, especially pressure coming from an authority figure. Sherry would be very upset at this point, but she would simply quit talking as she sat and stewed over what was happening. If she tried to argue, I'd say, "Listen, whatever gave you the idea that you're in charge here? I'm the teacher, and I run this class. You don't have a choice. I'm doing this for the good of everyone, so everyone of you might as well get used to it."

By this time, something strange would happen. Danny, in the back of the class who had been benefiting from this exercise, would say, "Mr. Hawkins, I don't want any more points. It's okay if I fail."

I'd smile and say, "Danny, that's very noble of you to be willing to fail so others can succeed, but I'm not going to let anyone fail." I'd then address the entire class and they'd all groan and say it wasn't fair what I was doing. I'd reply, "Fair? How is it fair that some of you score "A's" while others fail? Don't you care about those who don't do as well as you. After all, fair is when everyone can make the same score. How is someone who scores a 97 and someone else a 32 fair?! I can't believe you all are so selfish!"

Those who had been quiet before began to speak up and say it wasn't fair to take points from those who studied to give to those who didn't study. The entire class was upset with me now, including Danny!

I'd then put my hands up to calm them down and say, "If you all are so upset, let's talk about this for a minute." They would settle down, and I would take on a more relaxed demeanor, which created a truce for a few moments.

"Let me ask you a few things. Sherry, do you think it was fair I took those points from you to give to Danny?"

She would emphatically answer, "NO!"

I'd then turn to Danny and say, "In the beginning, you liked it when I was giving points to you, so what changed?"

Danny would say, "It just got embarrassing that I was causing so much of a problem for everyone else."

I'd turn back to Sherry and the others who had originally earned an "A" and ask them all, "Are you going to work as hard to get an 'A' next time?"

They'd answer in unison, "Why should we?"

"Danny, what about you? Are you going to work any harder to score more points for the next quiz? That way I won't have to take so many points from everybody else?"

He'd answer, "What does it matter if you're going to do the same thing?"

I'd look at the clock, and the class period was almost up. So, I'd say, "Class, this lesson today was about socialism. What you just experienced is socialism where I took from those who achieved to give to those who didn't. I called it being fair. Was it fair?"
The class would shake their heads no.

"As the teacher in this lesson I represented the government. I had the authority to take however many points I wanted, and I could force you to accept it. When you complained, I took points anyway, and there was nothing you could do about it. That's how governments act under socialism, and the more extreme the socialism, like communism, the more they will force their citizens against their will. Communist governments will even kill their own citizens to get them to obey."

I'd then finish by saying, "I have good news for you. Be thankful I'm a capitalist and not a socialist. That means you all get to keep your original scores. Sherry, you get to keep your 97. The rest of you get all your points back. Danny, you also get your original score back too."

I'd then look at Sherry who was still showing frustration and say, "Are you okay with keeping what you earned?"

She'd say, "Yes." She still wouldn't smile, though.

"Danny, are you okay with keeping your 32?"

He'd say he was.

"Class let this be a lesson to you. Be careful when someone says they want to make things fair by taking from some to give to others. Now that you know what socialism is, class dismissed."

*   *   *

Socialism is based on greed and jealousy. One person is jealous of what another person has earned. That jealousy leads to a misguided belief that the person who earned is not worthy of what he has because his wealth was achieved, or is used, in a nefarious way. This false belief justifies their belief that the government needs to take from those that have earned to give to those who have not in the name of equality. They think of the government as Robin Hood.

However, Robin Hood did not take from the rich to give to the poor. He took from the government to give to the poor because the Sheriff of Nottingham (the government) was taking too much in taxes from the people.

Some people and churches go so far as to say Jesus Christ taught socialism, and if he were walking the earth today, he would be a Democrat. Well, so far we've seen the Democrats have rejected 9 commandments, so let's take a look at the words of Jesus Christ and see if he would agree or disagree with them on their stance on the 10th commandment.

Take a look at Luke 12:13-15. *"And one of the company said unto him, Master, speak to my brother, that he divide the inheritance with me.*
14 And he said unto him, Man, who made me a judge or a divider over you?
15 And he said unto them, Take heed, and beware of covetousness: for a man's life consisteth not in the abundance of the things which he possesseth."

When Jesus was asked to redistribute the wealth, he warned the young man of the 10th commandment. Do not be jealous or envious of what others have

77

because life is not about how much you can acquire. The idea of wealth redistribution is a violation of God's Word, and Jesus Christ would have nothing to do with it.

One of the most misquoted verses in the Bible has to do with the relationship between money and evil. How many times have you heard someone say "money is the root of all evil"?

I Timothy actually says, *"For the love of money is the root of all evil: which while some coveted after, they have erred from the faith, and pierced themselves through with many sorrows."*

Money is not evil, but the LOVE of money is. What's the difference? When one covets money, they are placing money over God. They believe happiness is found through the accumulation of wealth. They will sometimes ignore God's Word and violate it by mistreating people to get more money. They believe money will solve all their problems. The man who thinks like that is wrong, and the man who seeks to get what he has through redistribution of wealth is also wrong.

Let's take a look at this parable that Jesus gave the people in Matthew 25:14-30.

"For the kingdom of heaven is as a man travelling into a far country, who called his own servants, and delivered unto them his goods.
15 And unto one he gave five talents, to another two, and to another one; to every man according to his several ability; and straightway took his journey.
16 Then he that had received the five talents went and traded with the same, and made them other five talents.
17 And likewise he that had received two, he also gained other two.
18 But he that had received one went and digged in the earth, and hid his lord's money.

19 After a long time the lord of those servants cometh, and reckoneth with them.

20 And so he that had received five talents came and brought other five talents, saying, Lord, thou deliveredst unto me five talents: behold, I have gained beside them five talents more.

21 His lord said unto him, Well done, thou good and faithful servant: thou hast been faithful over a few things, I will make thee ruler over many things: enter thou into the joy of thy lord.

22 He also that had received two talents came and said, Lord, thou deliveredst unto me two talents: behold, I have gained two other talents beside them.

23 His lord said unto him, Well done, good and faithful servant; thou hast been faithful over a few things, I will make thee ruler over many things: enter thou into the joy of thy lord.

24 Then he which had received the one talent came and said, Lord, I knew thee that thou art an hard man, reaping where thou hast not sown, and gathering where thou hast not strawed:

25 And I was afraid, and went and hid thy talent in the earth: lo, there thou hast that is thine.

26 His lord answered and said unto him, Thou wicked and slothful servant, thou knewest that I reap where I sowed not, and gather where I have not strawed:

27 Thou oughtest therefore to have put my money to the exchangers, and then at my coming I should have received mine own with usury.

28 Take therefore the talent from him, and give it unto him which hath ten talents.

29 For unto every one that hath shall be given, and he shall have abundance: but from him that hath not shall be taken away even that which he hath.

30 And cast ye the unprofitable servant into outer darkness: there shall be weeping and gnashing of teeth.

Here we have the owner of a business who was wealthy and had three employees. The boss gave his three employees some money according to how responsible they had proven themselves to be. Notice, he gave them different amounts. The more responsible and diligent they were, the more he gave them. Jesus did not condemn the owner for this.

The first employee doubled his boss' money and, as a result, the boss gave him more with which to work. The second employee was also honored because he too had doubled the owner's investment.

However, the least responsible one hid the money out of fear. His fear caused him to do nothing but waste his opportunity. Not only did he waste his opportunity, but at the same time, he angered his boss for blaming his fear on the owner. So, the owner lets him know he was more than just lazy; he was corrupt, too. He had actually cost the owner money.

He was reminded that, at the very least, he could have put the money in a savings account at the bank to draw interest.

Jesus did not condemn the owner or the two employees who made money. Instead, he rewarded those two employees. The one who was wrong was the one who did nothing to increase the amount of money he was entrusted with - to the point that what he had was taken from him and given to the one who had the most already. Not only did Jesus not take from the haves and give to the have nots, he took from the one who had the least and gave to the one who had the most.

Jesus is saying it is wrong to reward laziness and corruption that comes with waste. He rewarded faith and investment. He who creates wealth is rewarded, and he who squanders what has been given to him is condemned. Through this parable, Jesus Christ is showing that free enterprise is a good thing.

Did you notice in the parable above that not even money changers (banks) were a bad thing? Some say Jesus did not like the money changers, institutions like banks and Wall Street, because he threw them out of the Temple. They were thrown out of the Temple not because they were money changers, but because they were set up in his House, the temple.

He never threw them out of anywhere else; as a matter of fact, he did not condemn money changers for what they did, just where they did it.

Where is the party?

The Republican Party believes in free enterprise and capitalism. Nowhere did Jesus Christ condemn free enterprise and making money. He actually said it was to be rewarded in his parables. Free enterprise and capitalism do not violate the 10th commandment.

The Democrat Party has continued to accept the leftist position of socialism, which calls for wealth redistribution and is based on breaking the 10th commandment by having the government take what belongs to someone else for the purpose of "equality." It also teaches that people are victims of the rich and powerful, life is unfair, and only the Democrat Party can give those they declare victims what they want.

The party has been taken over by leftists masquerading as Democrats of old. Most Democrat voters are not leftists (Marxists), but the leadership of the party has proven themselves to be either leftists or fellow travelers with them to the point the Democrat Party is not not the party of your parents or grandparents. Any way you look at it, the Democrat Party violates all 10 of the commandments without exception. It's time your politics aligns with your faith.

Some people continue to vote for their leaders simply because their parents and grandparents were Democrats. The Democrat Party has moved drastically left over the years, and they are no longer the party of your parents and grandparents. Would they vote for people who opposed all 10 of God's commandments?

Some people vote for leaders who oppose the Ten Commandments because they think they are being more compassionate and a good person by supporting those who reject what God says about the issues. There are natural consequences to violating God's commandments. We cannot break God's laws and then expect things to work out.

The consequences for breaking God's law are always bad and never good, no matter how much we wish they were or deny God. It is impossible to avoid the bad consequences - not because God hates us or loves punishing us, but simply because of the natural consequences of defying God who wants us to have life and life more abundant. God does not go around seeking whom he may devour. As it says in I Peter 5:8, *"Be sober, be vigilant; because your adversary the devil, as a roaring lion, walketh about, seeking whom he may devour."*

Remember, they are called the Ten Commandments, not the Ten Suggestions. Where do you stand? Are you with God or against God?

Chapter 14

Truth

What is truth?

Is there truth, or is truth relative and up to individuals to find truth on their own? Humanism says that truth is relative to your own experiences; whereas the Judeo- Christian ethic says God is truth and God defines truth. If, as a Christian, my truth conflicts with leftists' truth, then the leftist says I'm wrong. However, using their own misguided logic, how can they say my truth is wrong if all truth is relative to our own experience? With the logic of the left, they cannot say I am wrong, but they do anyway.

Can I say the left is wrong? Yes, because my truth is based on God's truth, and God's truth is truth. Can they dismiss my truth because they say it is not based on my experience but on what is written in an ancient book? No, because my experience is that the ancient book and the salvation God gave freely to me is true. Therefore, the left cannot deny me my truth.

Yet, they fight against it all the time. They fight in the political arena, and they fight in the arena of the church. Does your church proclaim or deny the Ten Commandments? If your church proclaims the Ten Commandments, then you are in a good church. If your church only proclaims some of the Ten Commandments but denies others, well then, you may want to look into that. If your church denies all 10 of the 10 commandments, then you may want to leave that church because they are not worshipping God.

If you're a Christian, the same holds true for your political party. If your party supports the Ten Commandments, then you're in a good party. If your party only supports some of the Ten Commandments, then you may want to look into that. If your party denies 10 of the Ten Commandments, then you may want to leave that party because they are not reflecting God's values. Instead, they are shamelessly defying God.

If your party comes before God's Word, then please don't call yourself a Christian. As it says in Luke 16:27, *"No servant can serve two masters: for either he will hate the one and love the other; or else he will hold to the one, and despise the other. Ye cannot serve God and mammon."*

Make your choice: God or party? Truth or error?

In case you're in a church that doesn't teach the Word of God, let me remind you what it says about truth.

"Thou art near, O LORD; and all thy commandments are truth." (Psalm 119:151)

God is truth! If one rejects God, then truth is also rejected. If truth is rejected, then man must devise another way of ascertaining the truth. The problem is, there is no other way. John 14:6 says, *"Jesus saith unto him, I am the way, the truth, and the life: no man cometh unto the Father, but by me."*

Philosophies that deny God while they search for truth search in vain. *"Ever learning, and never able to come to the knowledge of the truth."* (II Timothy 3:7)

Humanism has changed the truth of God into a lie.

"Who changed the truth of God into a lie, and worshipped and served the creature more than the Creator, who is blessed for ever. Amen." (Romans 1:25)

84

How does one obtain truth?

"Who will have all men to be saved, and to come unto the knowledge of the truth." (I Timothy 2:4)

Your political party won't save you. Jesus Christ did not come to save us politically, but spiritually. The one disciple who was looking for a political savior was named Judas, and he betrayed Jesus for money and power. His love for money and power overshadowed his love for the Son of God.

Judas was looking for social justice. He had followed a leader he believed would be the next King of the Jews, who would overthrow the occupation of the Romans. He gave Jesus lip service, but his heart was looking for political answers instead of spiritual.

When a political party rejects the Ten Commandments, all 10 of them, but then tries to say that Jesus Christ agrees with them, that party is just like Judas. They are looking for political answers and rejecting God and His Word.

Salvation is not found in the Republican Party either. Keeping the Ten Commandments does not save a person. Living as close as possible might make your life easier since you won't be suffering the natural consequences of sin, but keeping the Ten Commandments cannot save you.

For a person to be saved, that person must first realize he or she is lost. If you're lost, you're searching for a way out. A way home. A way to make sense of it all. People try different things to get them unlost in an effort to feel like everything will be alright. Many leftists are leftists because they're searching for a place to belong and a purpose for their life.

Are you trying to find a reason and purpose for your life? Many try to find purpose in causes and movements, but there is still an emptiness that needs to be addressed.

If that's how you feel, well then, that's a pretty good sign you're lost. You need peace in your life. You need understanding. You need hope.

Peace comes from God through Jesus Christ.

'Grace unto you, and peace, from God our Father and the Lord Jesus Christ." (II Thessalonians 1:2)

Then Jesus gives us understanding, as it says in I John 5:20: *"And we know that the Son of God is come, and hath given us an understanding, that we may know him that is true, and we are in him that is true, even in his Son Jesus Christ. This is the true God, and eternal life."*

Finally you can have hope, as it says in I Peter 1:21, *"Who by him do believe in God, that raised him up from the dead, and gave him glory; that your faith and hope might be in God."*

Would you like to have your eyes opened to the spiritual world? I'm not talking about ghosts and goblins. I'm talking about the knowledge and understanding of God. Ask yourself this question. What must I do to be saved?

The first thing you need to know is God loves you. He really loves you in a way that will be unfathomable to you. Not all Christians love like they're supposed to. We're supposed to love like God loves; however, that requires Christians walking as close as possible with God, and we don't always do that. *"But God commendeth his love toward us, in that, while we were yet sinners, Christ died for us."* (Romans 5:8)

The good news is you don't have to clean up your life first. *"If we confess our sins, he is faithful and just to forgive us our sins, and to cleanse us from all unrighteousness."* (I John 1:9)

86

First, realize you are lost because there have been times in your life when you have done the wrong thing. Then ask Jesus Christ to forgive you for those sins and put your faith in Him to save you so that you may go to heaven when you die.

You see, being the Son of God, he was the only one ever that kept all of the Ten Commandments without breaking them even one time. Then, by willingly sacrificing himself on the cross, he paid the penalty for sin, which is death.

"For the wages of sin is death; but the gift of God is eternal life through Jesus Christ our Lord." (Romans 6:23)

Being God, he raised himself up the third day to overcome even death and finish his task of paying for the sins of everyone who would put their faith in him.

"For God so loved the world, that he gave his only begotten Son, that whosoever believeth in him should not perish, but have everlasting life." (John 3:16)

Then again, you can let your pride keep you from allowing Jesus Christ to bring your spirit to life and opening your eyes to a whole new world. If that's the case, keep searching for that elusive peace, understanding, and hope.

As it says in Joshua 24:15, "...choose you this day whom ye will serve..."

Choose now and choose wisely.

www.ingramcontent.com/pod-product-compliance
Lightning Source LLC
Chambersburg PA
CBHW062109040426
42336CB00042B/2841